BUILDING COI
DOCUMENTS

Using Microsoft Word 2007, 2010, and 2013

F. Mark Schiavone, Ph.D.

Sycamore Technical Press
www.sycamoretechnicalpress.com

Preface

Welcome to the world of the Microsoft Word power user! Power users create documents that go way beyond simple text with minimal formatting. We don't settle for a manually created table of contents or a colleague who thinks that in the 21st Century it is acceptable to print a 250 page document and make edits with a pencil. If you have not yet created a complex document, this book is the perfect entry point. Each topic will be covered beginning with first principles and will take you stepwise through the process of understanding, implementing, and managing each component that makes up a complex document. If you are already a power user of Microsoft Word and you're looking for additional insight you're still in the right place. The book covers extensive troubleshooting tips and the text is peppered with shortcuts and best practices you may not have known existed.

Not every complex document will contain every element type discussed in this book. Indeed, the nature of your work may only focus on documents that include a table of contents and perhaps the occasional appendix. In these cases feel free to skip the chapters that focus on elements you know you will not work with and instead center on the chapters that include pertinent information (such as working with templates in Chapter 5).

The book will focus on standard documents typical of a modern workplace. Not covered are topics that merge word processing with desktop publishing—for example brochures and advertisement layout. However, the chapter on graphics may provide the reader with useful information to create such documents.

Manual Conventions

Throughout this manual reference is made to various components of the software. Tabs, groups and command buttons appear in boldface type, for example, **OK** and **Font**. Keystrokes appear in boldface italic type, for example, ***Ctrl + V*** and ***Enter***. When possible, the words *select* and *choose* have been used in this manual to allow you the option of using either the mouse or keyboard. Throughout this manual you'll find the following helpful items:

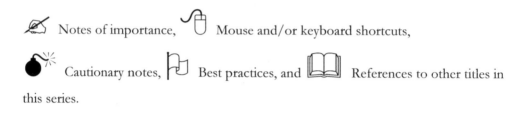 Notes of importance, Mouse and/or keyboard shortcuts, Cautionary notes, Best practices, and References to other titles in this series.

Table of Contents

Chapter 1 | Introduction to Complex Documents

A complex document, as the name suggests, involves more than simple text. They take the form of reports, policy statements, operating manuals, books, and the myriad of other document types that are essential products of the modern workplace. Such documents are typically scores of pages long and contain elements such as tables, figures, enforced styles, foot and endnotes, and cross references (which include tables of contents and indices).

What Makes a Document Complex?

A document is complex when it goes beyond just text and paragraph formatting. Weighing in at over 450 pages doesn't necessarily make a document complex. Instead, think of a complex document as having at least one of these attributes:

- Use of *styles*—either the built in styles or custom styles—to standardize the appearance of text and paragraphs or to denote major sections of the document (such as chapters, headings and subheadings).

- Use of *sections* to create changes in page orientation or to establish headers or footers which differ from section to section.

- Inclusion of *tables*. Tables are *not* constructed using tab stops but are cellular elements that have a structure that is different from regular text.

- Pictures, graphics, drawings, and/or equations—either as *in-line* elements that flow with the text stream or as *anchored* elements that force text to flow around them. Graphics may be inserted or *linked*. The latter meaning that if the original graphic changes it is also automatically updated in the document as well.

- Linked or inserted objects from other applications, such as a section of a Microsoft Excel worksheet or graph, or a slide from a Microsoft PowerPoint presentation. Like graphics, these objects may be inserted, *embedded* or *linked* to give you greater flexibility regarding how original source changes migrate (or not) into your document.

- References—which can include foot and end-notes, cross references, captions, one or more table of contents, and an index. Each of these elements exists as a dynamic field which is capable of automatically updating as the document evolves.

Any of these items when present in a Word document makes the document more complex than one containing simple text. The complexity isn't necessarily a drawback. Indeed, many of these elements bring a suite of powerful features that simplify working with them. This book will explore each of these elements in turn. Before we begin we will review some of the important approaches to working with complex documents and explain in detail how each of these elements works within the context of the document.

Essential Tools

As with any skill, mastery of the tools of the trade helps advance one to expert status and this is true of word processing as well. In the case of Microsoft Word, there are a few components that require deep understanding in order to competently work with complex documents. These include an understanding of the basic nature of a Microsoft Word document, understanding styles and their interplay with other elements such as the table of contents, cross references, and the Document Map, and understanding sections—which constitute the major until of organization in a Word document. We'll introduce these elements here and then go into greater detail in Chapters 2 through 8.

Understanding the Structure of a Word Document

Microsoft Word was the first major word processing application to structure documents as a collection of objects. In computer programming, an object is an entity that exposes properties and methods and is frequently a member of a greater hierarchy. This is true of a Word document and Microsoft Word arranges documents into a three-tier hierarchy: characters, paragraphs, and sections. The lowest level of organization is the character and at this level Microsoft Word isn't much different from any other word processing application such as WordPerfect. Each character in a word or phrase may have different attributes applied to it, so it's possible in either word processor to create words like **t**h*is*. Each letter in the example is a different font or font attribute (property) such as **bold**, *italic*, or underline. The next two levels up are where the differences between Microsoft Word and other word processing applications begin to appear. In Word, the sentences that make up a paragraph (paragraphs are denoted as ending in a carriage return) all share similar attributes such as line spacing, indentation, and widow/orphan control. You can see a simple example of this by positioning the insertion point anywhere in the center of a paragraph that occupies more than a few lines and changing the line spacing from single to double space. In Microsoft Word the *entire* paragraph adopts the new line spacing property. In WordPerfect the new line spacing will only take effect *downstream* from the insertion point—reflecting the fact that WordPerfect is still character-based, even at the level of a paragraph.

The third level in this object-hierarchy is the section and here is where Microsoft Word can create problems, especially for users who have migrated from WordPerfect. Sections organize one or more pages into similar units. A good example of a section is a book chapter where you want the page numbering in a running footer to include the chapter title as well. Each chapter must constitute a separate section to achieve this goal. Another case where sections are required is whenever the page orientation (or page source for a printer) is different. So even within a single chapter, if you have one or more pages which must be arranged in landscape orientation, you need to create separate sections for each change in page orientation.

Those three levels of organization make up an entire Word document. Luckily the character and paragraph levels are pretty intuitive, especially for regular uses of word processors. Sections can introduce problems and although we will go into more detail for each of these entities, we will pay particular attention to sections, the problems which may arise when using them, and troubleshooting tips for correcting such problems.

Understanding Styles

A style is simply a named set of character or paragraph attributes which may be applied to portions of a document. Word recognizes three types of styles: character, paragraph, and linked styles (which is a hybrid character-paragraph style whose application depends upon whether a word or a paragraph has been selected). More recent versions of Word extend the concept of styles to include styles for numbered or bulleted lists as well as for tables. In these cases, the notion of a predefined set of format attributes remains the same.

We will delve into styles in more detail in Chapter 3, but for the moment if one were to summarize why styles are important in a complex document it would be these points:

- Styles are quick to apply and thus save the author much time while working on a document.

- Consistent use of styles aids in the enforcement of a standard look and feel in a document. For example, by using a paragraph style that specifies the amount of space before and after each paragraph for all body text you dispense with the need to add one or more paragraph marks between paragraphs. Since styles are easily modified, a change in such a parameter immediately cascades throughout the document.

- Styles can be associated with *outline levels* and these feed directly into the organization and structure of such elements as a table of contents, complex page numbering, and the Document Map.

- Wherever a style is applied Word is capable of tracking that location. Hence, styles can serve as points of reference when applying cross references. Styles may be the focal point of a Find operation as well.

Understanding Sections

As previously mentioned, a section represents the highest level of organization in a Word document. Sections basically map to page attributes with the exception that a section may contain one-to-many pages. Unlike some word processors, it isn't possible in Word to just open a header or footer on a particular page and change the contents so the header or footer is different *just* for that page. Any change made to the header or footer affects *all* pages in that section. The same is true for changes in page orientation as well. You'll work with sections under any of the following conditions:

- You need headers or footers to be different in places throughout your document. Common situations include documents that include chapter titles in the page header or footer, or places such as a preface or appendix where the numbering scheme changes.

- Your document contains one or more pages that are oriented differently than the rest of the document. The majority of pages may be in portrait orientation but in several places you need to change to landscape to manage very large tables or graphics.

- Columns (as opposed to regular block text) will be applied to one or more locations in a document.

- You need to change physical attributes of the printed page in one or more locations within a document. These changes include different page size, different page margins, or different paper sources for a printer.

By themselves sections wouldn't be too difficult to work with. The problem is a nasty little property called *same as previous* that is applied by default when you add a new section to a document. This attribute works fine for simple documents that may contain multiple sections but use the same header or footer style throughout. If you've ever experienced situations where a change you made to some section attribute (like modifying one header or footer or changing the page orientation of one page) cascades upwards through your document, you've been stung by the *same as previous* attribute. We'll discuss how to work with this property in detail in Chapter 4.

Essential Views

Before we tour the components of a complex document it would be useful to discuss some of the views, dialog boxes, and panes that provide useful functionality when working with documents.

Microsoft Word offers 5 separate views when working with a document. The sixth, **Print Preview** isn't included in this list as you can only view a document in that mode, while the other 5 offer some editing functionality. The default view, **Print Layout**, is the view used throughout this book. This is the what-you-see-it-what-you-get (WYSIWYG) view of the early word processors.

In Word it shows you exactly how your text and other elements will flow across pages. The available views are selected by either choosing them from the **Document Views** group located on the **View** tab, or by selecting the view from a cluster of view buttons on the lower right corner of the **Status Bar**. The following table summarizes the views:

View	Description
Print Layout	Presents the document as it will be formatted on the printed page. If **Show/Hide** is enabled, some text may be displaced as hidden text and field codes are also displayed in line with the text in this mode.
Full Screen Reading	Removes all clutter from the screen and presents the document in a two-page spread, much like reading a book. This view is optimized for reading, although simple edits to the text are supported.
Web Layout	Formats the page as it would appear if viewed in a web browser.
Outline	Emphasizes the structure of your document by creating a hierarchical view based on use of the built-in heading styles (or styles you create and assign an *outline level*). Headers and footers, graphics, and other elements do not appear in this view.
Draft	A no-frills view that emphasizes the text stream. Section attributes such as headers or footers, changes in page orientation, etc. do not appear.

Show/Hide

One important element in the majority of these views is **Show/Hide** which, when enabled, displays such non-printing characters as the paragraph mark (¶), spaces between words (·), and tabs (→). The utility of working with **Show/Hide** enabled is that you can see each instance of a paragraph ending or a tab in the document. When using the **Format Painter** to quickly copy paragraph formatting having **Show/Hide** turned on is essential. The drawback to working with **Show/Hide** is when your document includes hidden fields such as those used in tagging index entries, your document flow really isn't an accurate reflection of the text flow since the display of this hidden text affects text spacing. In these cases it is a simple matter of toggling **Show/Hide** when you are undergoing the last checks in a document prior to finalizing it.

How to Toggle Show/Hide

Step 1.   From the **Home** tab, in the **Paragraph** group, choose ¶.

The keyboard shortcut for this toggle is *Ctrl* * (control shift 8).

The Document Map (2007/2010)

Think of the document map as a real-time table of contents for your document. As you work with styles such as the built-in *Heading 1* or *Heading 3*, create paragraph styles with **Outline Levels**, or mark text to be included in a Table of Contents, the **Document Map** updates to show you the hierarchical structure of your document. If you select an item in the **Document Map**, the **Print Layout** view jumps to that location in the document, making this pane a great tool for quickly navigating through your document.

The document map may also be used to move entire sections of a document. Simply click and drag a document map entry to move it to another location. To open the **Document Map**:

How to Open the Document Map (2007/2010)

Step 1. From the **View** tab in the **Show/Hide** group, choose **Document Map**. By default the **Document Map** opens in **Thumbnails** view. Although this view is useful for moving between pages, it does not reflect the organizational hierarchy if you are working with **Outline Levels**.

Step 2. To change views, from the drop down box on the **Document Map** pane, select **Document Map**. The **Document Map** will appear similar to the following:

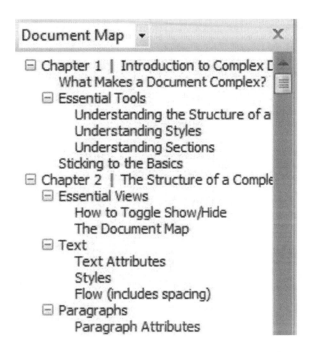

When the **Document Map** initially opens it displays every paragraph style associated with an **Outline Level**. These are discussed in greater detail later in this Chapter but know that outline levels feed into the organization of any table of contents you may include in the document. You can expand or collapse individual items in the **Document Map** by clicking on the small **Expand** or **Collapse** squares to the left of an entry. If you right-click on the **Document Map** you can select one of the *Heading* entries (Heading 1 through Heading 9) to conduct a bulk collapse or expand operation. For example, choosing **Heading 1** from the shortcut menu would collapse the document map to only show paragraphs in the **Heading 1** style. If you're using this style to denote chapter titles this essentially collapses the map to only display your chapter headings.

The document map makes it easy to collapse all chapters except the one you are working on (collapse all levels, then select the **Expand** control for the current chapter). Configuring the document map in this way reduces clutter, yet lets you quickly see the overall structure of the current chapter in your document.

The Object Browser (2007/2010)

Word offers a subtle tool known as the **Object Browser** to help you quickly move between pages, sections (the subject of Chapter 4), or between objects of various types. As an example you can use the **Object Browser** to step through each table in a document in order to ensure consistency between all tables. The **Object Browser** is part of the vertical scroll bar associated with the document viewing area. It is available in all document views except **Full Screen Reading**. The **Object Browser**, located at the lower portion of the vertical scroll bar, appears as follows:

The double-arrow controls are previous and next object, respectively while the dot opens the **Select Object Browser** menu. When set to browse by page (which is the default), the double arrows appear black. If the **Object Browser** is set to any other object type, these arrows change to blue—a subtle clue that you are not browsing by page.

In Word 2013 **Find** and **Advanced Find** offer some functionality that replaces the **Object Browser**. This is discussed on page 218.

How to Use the Object Browser (2007/2010)

Step 1.   If you wish to browse by page, first ensure that the double arrow controls are black and if so, simply select either the previous page (double arrow up) or next page (double arrow down) control. If these controls are not black or if you wish to browse by another object type proceed with this procedure.

Step 2.   Select the **Select Object Browser** dot. A menu of graphic options will appear. Floating the mouse over a graphic will produce a tool tip that names the object. Use the following table as a guide to understanding these choices.

Object Browser Options

Browse by	Description
Table	Steps between tables.
Graphic	Steps between graphics (any type).
Heading	Moves between any style associated with Heading levels one through ten.
Edits	Moves to the last 3 edits in the document.
Find	Opens the **Find and Replace** dialog and activates the **Find** tab. Once you have established a find condition you can close the dialog box and use the double arrow-up (find previous) or double arrow-down (find next) controls.
Go to	Opens the **Find and Replace** dialog and activates the **Go To** tab. You may choose many of the objects recognized by the **Object Browser**, but **Go To** allows you to specify a numbered item. For example, to jump 4 tables ahead or 10 pages back in a document.
Page	Browse one page forward or backward at a time. This is the default behavior for the **Object Browser**. Select this option if you wish to reset the control.
Section	Step between each section break in the document.
Comment	Move between comments. Useful when working with multi-user documents.
Footnote	Jump between footnotes.
Endnote	Jump between endnotes.
Field	Move between any type of *field*. Fields are used in Word to create cross references, index entries, etc.

The Navigation Pane (2013)

In more recent version of Microsoft Word, the **Navigation Pane** replaces the **Document Map,** although conceptually both devices permit quick navigation through a document. The big difference between the two is that the **Navigation Pane** incorporates the **Find** and **Object Browser** into the pane's options.

How to Open the Navigation Pane (2013)

In addition to the formal procedure outlined below, clicking on the page count in the **Status Bar** or pressing *Ctrl F* will open the **Navigation Pane**.

Step 1.   On the **View** tab, in the **Show** group, choose **Navigation pane**.

Step 2.   To change views, select either **Headings** (browse by heading style and outline levels), **Page** (browse by thumbnail)**,** or **Results** (browse by search results).

 When you use the **Navigation Pane** to browse by **Headings**, it behaves identically to the way its replacement, the **Document Map** works. See page 7 for details.

Reveal Formatting

Reveal formatting summarizes the attributes being applied to the current location in your document. It recognizes Word's three-level hierarchy of objects and thus the **Reveal Formatting** pane is divided into sections titled **Font, Paragraph**, and **Section**. For each attribute there is a hyperlink that will take you directly to the dialog box responsible for that attribute. This pane was originally added to Microsoft Word to help former users of WordPerfect get accustomed to the lack of reveal codes.

This facility was introduced a few versions back and unfortunately has been pushed into the world of obscure Word task panes—there isn't a direct way to view **Reveal Formatting**.

How to Open to Reveal Formatting Pane

Step 1.   Position the insertion point where you wish to inspect the formatting and press *Shift F1*. The **Reveal Formatting** pane will appear similar to the following:

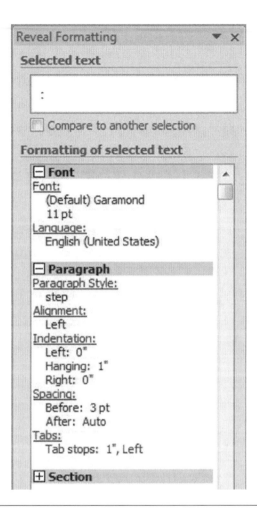

 The alternative (and not intuitive) route to open **Reveal Formatting** is to select the **Dialog Expander** in the **Styles** group. At the bottom of the **Styles** pane, choose **Style Inspector**. At the bottom of the **Style Inspector**, select **Reveal Formatting**. If desired, close the **Style Inspector** and the **Styles** Pane.

Apply Styles

This is another useful dialog box that Microsoft has decided to hide. In earlier versions of Microsoft Word there existed a style drop down box on the **Format** toolbar. You could activate this device from the keyboard by pressing *Ctrl Shift S*, type the name of a style, press *Enter* and continue typing. Using the **Styles** group on the **Home** tab requires use of the mouse, which for power keyboardist is an unacceptable break in the flow of typing. If you need to quickly change styles while not leaving the keyboard, the **Apply Styles** dialog is your solution.

Using *Ctrl Shift S* still activates the style dropdown, but it appears now in a floating, always on top, dockable dialog box, similar to the following:

The original functionality of the drop down box is retained. If you type the name of a style, once it appears in the drop down box, pressing *Enter* will apply that style at the current cursor location and return control to the document.

Other authors would probably suggest alternative or additional dialog boxes and panes to open while working with a complex document. It's this author's experience that at a minimum the **Document Map** (2007), **Navigation Pane** (2010/2013), **Reveal Formatting**, and **Apply Styles** are essential when generating the original text or conducting format edits to any large document.

Sticking to the Basics

Each new version of Microsoft Word seems to include larger style and format galleries, templates, themes and other bundled features that really map back to a set of styles or section attributes bundled together. One thing we will not do in this book is to take an extensive tour of all the built-in styles and templates. Instead we will learn how to modify existing styles and templates, and to create new ones. These skills are far preferable than just knowing that there are over 20 built-in themes or that the **Styles** group on the **Home** tab contains 25 predefined styles. The assumption here is that you, or your organization, is interested in creating documents that reflect your style, not that of Microsoft. So with the expressed purpose of learning how to customize Word to enable you to create a complex document we'll proceed along a unique path. Along the way you'll be introduced to dialog boxes that give you great flexibility in creating, modifying, and managing these essential elements of a complex document.

Good File Management Techniques

Your complex document will begin to reflect the many hours of hard work that you and/or others have invested. More recent versions of Microsoft Office have gotten much better at faithfully recovering from unpredictable disasters such as an unannounced shut down of Microsoft Word, or the complete loss of power on your computer. Still, it is imprudent to allow Word to exclusively manage the versions of your document. Large organizations may routinely create restore points for all documents and locally you can configure Windows to create similar restore points. Before embarking on a large document project, you should ensure that **AutoSave** settings are appropriate.

Another, parallel approach is to routinely save a working document using a scheme that notes a version number or production date in the file name. By essentially using **Save as** at the end of each day you create an audit trail of every day's work. In the event of a wholesale failure of the most recent document you're able to recover the previous day's version (thus keeping loses to one day's effort). For mission critical work you may consider a finer degree of granularity by saving an important document with a date/time stamp in the file name, thus limiting potential loses to a few hours at best.

It is also useful to consider creating backup copies of a complex document before large scale changes are made. Saving a document before the final check of headers and footers, or before the insertion of a table or contents or an index are all good ways to ensure that you can roll back to a previous version in the event something goes wrong. And of course, save a copy of your document before sending it to a printer or uploading it to a remote printer or publisher.

How to Adjust Auto Recovery Settings

This feature ensures that Word creates a backup of your open documents every so often. Although on by default, it is a good idea to make sure it is enabled and saves at an appropriate frequency to meet your needs.

Step 1.   Select the **Office** button (2007), or the **File** tab (2010/2013) then choose **Word Options** (2007) or **Options** (2010/2013).

Step 2.   Move to the **Save** area. Ensure that **Save Auto Recovery files every XX minutes** is checked. Adjust the **Minutes** control to an appropriate value.

Step 3.   Choose **OK**.

The default **Auto Recovery** time is 10 minutes. Setting it lower will affect Words responsiveness as it pauses more frequently to backup documents. Increasing the time increment raises the potential that you lose more work in the event of an unexpected shut down.

How to Recover a Document

If **Auto Recovery** is enabled and you experience an unexpected shut down, Word will open the **Document Recovery Pane** when you restart Word.

Step 1.   Restart Word.

Step 2.   For each document listed in the **Document Recovery Pane**, locate the **Auto Recover** version and open it.

Step 3.   Ensure that the document is in order, then save it using a different file name. In most cases, the **Auto Recovered** version will be the most up-to-date.

Step 4.   When done, close the **Document Recovery Pane**.

Chapter 2 | The Structure of a Complex Document

In the first Chapter we were introduced to a list of the items that if present in a Word document, justify thinking of the document as being complex. In this Chapter we delve a bit deeper into these elements and survey their basic attributes and discuss how each relates to the greater document. For many of these elements we will go into even greater detail in a series of Chapters, each dedicated to an important item such as working with styles, sections, graphics and figures.

Text

Text is obviously the fundamental component of any document. Text consists of the lowest unit of organization in a Word document—the character. As such this element has attributes, styles, and can be thought of as having *flow* in a document.

Text Attributes

The attributes of a character map directly to those options available from the **Font** group on the **Home** tab, and those settings fall into two categories: **Font** and **Character Spacing**. The **Font** attributes focus on which font to use, the point size, style (here meaning bold, italic, underline, etc.), and special effects such as super- or sub-script, strike-through, or small caps. These attributes are so fundamental to word processing that they do not warrant deeper discussion in this book.

Character spacing is controlled by opening the **Font** dialog box (either use the **Dialog Expander** on the **Font** group or press *Ctrl d*) and moving to the **Character Spacing** tab in earlier versions of Word or in Word 2010 and later—the **Advanced** tab. The options available are explained in the following table.

Advanced Font Attributes

Attribute	Description
Scale	Alters the size/shape of characters horizontally.
Spacing	Adds (expand) or removes (condense) spacing between characters. This adjustment is conducted in tenths of a point.
Position	Moves characters above or below the baseline that is used to vertically align characters. Positioning defaults to increments of whole points but you can enter decimal values as well.
Kerning for Fonts	Applies *kerning* for the font when it is above the specified font size.

 A *point* in word processing and desk top publishing is $1/72^{nd}$ of an inch. Generally, readable text falls within the 9-12 point range. Larger point sizes are used for headings while smaller point sizes are frequently used in foot and end notes.

Styles

As previously mentioned, there are three types of styles with one being a character style. Any of the attributes of character formatting discussed above can be specified and saved as a character style. In the illustration below, two character styles are noted by the presence of a bold lowercase letter a in the list of available styles from the **Style Pane**.

Subtle Emphasis	**a**
Subtle Reference	**a**

Character-based styles are useful when you need to apply more than one formatting attribute at a time, or if you wish to be able to quickly search on such formatted text using **Advanced Find**. We will discuss the creation and management of character styles in Chapter 3. If you position the cursor within text formatted in a character style and evoke the **Format Painter** you can transfer that style to any text you then click on.

Paragraphs

In a word processing document, a paragraph is a stream of text that ends in a *hard return* (earlier usage also recognized the term *carriage return*). This involves embedding a special symbol (usually a carriage return/line feed combination) in the text stream. In electronic documents, the following entities are also considered paragraphs (since they end with a hard return):

- Headings.
- Entries in a numbered or bulleted list.
- Isolated instances of the paragraph mark character (¶) without other characters. Typically these occur when a keyboardist presses the **Enter** key several times between other elements in a document.

When you use the **Format Painter** to copy paragraph styles you need to select either the entire paragraph or if **Show/Hide** is enabled, select the ending paragraph mark before activating the **Format Painter**. If it isn't clear to Word that you're selecting a paragraph the **Format Painter** will transfer character styles instead.

Paragraph Attributes

Because a paragraph is a self-contained structural unit, the attributes associated with paragraphs tend to speak to the structural aspect. Common paragraph attributes include line spacing, indentation, spacing before or after the paragraph, and overall alignment. Within these confines the text that makes up the individual sentences (for multiple-line paragraphs) flows.

Word includes additional attributes, some of which are available from the **Format** group while the majority of the specialty features are only accessible from the **Paragraph** dialog, accessed by choosing the **Dialog Expander** on the **Paragraph** group. These additional attributes are discussed in the following table:

Advanced Paragraph Attributes

Attribute	Description
Indentation	Adjusts the left and/or right margin for the paragraph. This setting does not affect the page margin. It also controls whether the first line in a paragraph is treated differently (first line indent vs. hanging indent).
Spacing	Controls both the spacing between lines within the paragraph and/or the spacing before and/or after the paragraph. Line spacing may be specified as units of the current point size (e.g. double spacing) or in fractions of a point. Spacing before and after a paragraph is always specified in points.
Pagination	**Widow/Orphan** - enabled by default, prevents a paragraph's last line from spilling over to the next page (widow) or the first line of a paragraph from appearing at the bottom of a page (orphan). In Word, this setting is on by default. **Keep with Next** - Enforces a rule specifying that a paragraph always stays with the next paragraph. Typically applied to headings and captions so they always appear immediately before the next paragraph. **Keep Lines Together** ensures that all lines within the paragraph stay on the same page. **Page Break Before** - always adds a page break before the paragraph. Useful when a particular paragraph must always begin at the top of a page.

The page break used by Word to ensure that paragraphs maintain these attributes *are not* hard page breaks (created when you type ***Ctrl Enter***). Manual page breaks should be avoided. Using attributes from the previous table are preferred.

In addition to the common and advanced paragraph attributes, Microsoft Word treats a number of additional attributes as being associated with the paragraph object.

Special Paragraph Attributes

Attribute	Description
Shading	Sets a background color for a paragraph. Shading runs from the paragraph left to right margin and will extend beyond the last sentence if the sentence does not end at the paragraph right margin.
Borders	A line or lines that may border the top, bottom, left, and/or right edge of the paragraph. Borders behave like shading and extend to the left and right paragraph margin. Borders remain tight to the top and bottom sentence while the space associated with **Spacing Before/After** runs beyond any borders.
Tabs	Tab stops are considered children of a paragraph, thus any tab stops set within a paragraph become a property of the paragraph.

Styles

A paragraph style will incorporate the elements discussed above, including special attributes such as shading and/or borders, plus whatever character attributes were in effect at the termination point of the paragraph. The illustration below indicates how paragraph styles are noted in the **Style Pane**.

Bullet List	¶
Caption	¶

Bullets and Numbering

A bulleted or numbered list is considered a special type of paragraph and as such, these elements are associated with their own style types. These styles are not available through the regular style dialog boxes—instead you work with them via the **Bullets, Numbering** or **Multilevel List** controls which are located in the **Paragraph** group on the **Home** tab. The following table outlines the differences between these three special paragraph types:

Bullets, Numbered, and Multilevel Lists

Type	Description
Bullet	A simple list of paragraphs that begin with a bullet icon. The bullet styles only control the type of bullet. You can use built-in bullets, symbols, or pictures. The indentation in a bullet list is an attribute of the paragraph and is controlled by using the **Ruler** or via the **Paragraph** dialog box.
Numbered	Similar to a bullet list, except the bullets are replaced by numbers (Arabic or Roman), text (example: One, Two, Three), or a custom combination (example: Step 5, Step 6, Step 7 or Item A, Item B, etc.).
Multilevel	A hybrid of either the bullet or numbered list style, this list type supports indentation and is used to create hierarchical lists. You can create such a list using the **Multilevel List** control, or by changing the **List Level** on an existing simple bullet or number list.

Warning: Bullet and number styles may not port to other document formats such as HTML or various electronic reader platforms. If you are interested in creating documents which are easily convertible into these other formats keep your bullet or number lists simple and avoid complexly formatted multilevel lists.

Flow

Text flow in a paragraph is less of an attribute and more of a behavior. For languages with left-right text flow, the individual words flow from top left across the space bound by the paragraph left and right margins, then via a *soft return* flow continues at the left margin on the next line and continues flow rightward. Paragraph settings such as **Alignment**, and **Hyphenation** help determine where the text flow breaks with a soft return upon reaching the right margin.

Text can also flow around embedded objects such as images, tables, or boxes. Controlling flow around these objects (in the majority of cases the default is to *not* flow around) is done by manipulating properties of the embedded object rather than the paragraph. When text does not flow around an object the object is treated like any other component of the text stream. For example, unless specific properties are set, a multi-row table will break if it is forced to span across a page break.

Sections

The section constitutes the highest level of organization in a Word document. The attributes of a section essentially map to attributes of the printed page—and include such elements as page size, margins and orientation. Headers and footers are also elements of a section and for users not familiar with sections in Microsoft Word, headers and footers can become an issue which will be addressed in Chapter 4.

By default, a Word document consists of a single section (section 1). The document can contain thousands of pages and still only have a single section until and unless one of the following conditions is met: (1) there is a change in page orientation, paper source or page margins, or (2) the contents of a header or footer must be different between items such as chapters (this includes changes to the numbering style), or (3) two or more text columns are required. If any of these conditions are true then the document must include additional sections.

The following illustration outlines how sections would be applied for a change in page orientation.

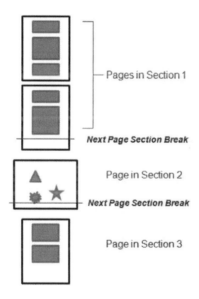

The pages in Section 1 have the *Portrait* page orientation attribute, and at the end of that section, a **Next Page Section Break** has been applied—thus creating Section 2. The second section has a single page (there could be many more) with the page orientation attribute of *Landscape*. At the end of the text and/or graphics in that section, a second **Next Page Section Break** has been applied, creating Section 3. The third section, like Section 1, uses the *Portrait* page orientation attribute.

It's important to note that a section *does not* map to a single page—although sections may certainly contain only a single page as in the illustration. However, adding additional pages in a section (either due to extra text or a forced manual page break) will insert a new page that inherits all attributes of the current section. Thus if a new page is created in Section 2 it will become a landscaped page. New pages in Sections 1 or 3 will become portrait in page orientation.

This behavior will be true for the other page attributes such as page margin and paper source (for printers).

When one first creates a new section in a Word document, it inherits the attributes from the previous section—exactly in the way that pressing the ***Enter*** key to create a new paragraph creates one that has inherited all of the paragraph attributes from the previous paragraph. To apply new page attributes to a newly created section you must manually modify them by generally making changes in the **Page Setup** group, located on the **Page Layout** tab.

This behavior will apply to the running headers and footers as well, *except* that the ability to inherit attributes from the previous entity can be toggled on or off for headers or footers. This feature is on by default and as we will discuss in Chapter 4 how one must take care when creating or inserting headers and/or footers that must be unique between sections.

Section Attributes

To recap, sections are responsible for the management of page-related attributes as indicated in the following table. There are no styles associated with sections, although by creating a *template*—discussed in Chapter 5—you can set default properties for Section 1 in a document. That Chapter will also discuss techniques for creating more sophisticated templates that contain multiple sections with differing page setup properties.

Section Attributes

Attribute	Description
Page Margins	The physical margins for the printed page. Note that within the limits of the current printer, you can extend paragraph margins beyond the page margins.
Page Orientation	Controls whether the page orientation is longer than wide (portrait), or wider than long (landscape).
Page Size	The physical dimensions of the paper used to print the page.
Page Source	When sending the document to a printer, this sets the tray the printer will use as the paper source. This setting is dependent upon the currently selected printer.
Columns	Used to define more than one vertical region for text flow. Many popular print sources such as newspapers and magazines utilize two or more columns per page. Section breaks are only enforced if you create a document that utilizes different column settings - for example to include a 3-column section in the middle of a 1-column document.
Header/Footer	These elements are always associated with sections, but their default **Keep with Next** property can modify their behavior so they inherit the settings of the previous section, even when other section attributes have been modified.

Additional Components

The previously discussed elements constitute the fundamental core of a complex document. The elements that follow embellish the document in a manner than raises the sophistication of the data presentation scheme and greatly improves the reader experience.

Tables

Prior to modern word processing, tables were created manually by arranging a series of tab stops which were used to align rows of text into vertical columns. Presently, tables are more sophisticated *cellular* objects that consist of discrete cells bounded by discrete rows and columns. These structures are recognized by the word processor as being objects which can have character and paragraph formatting applied on a cell by cell, row by row, column by column, or table by table basis.

Tables are sophisticated enough objects to warrant their own ribbon and tabs. When you insert a table or move to an existing one, the **Design** and **Layout** tab associated with the **Table Tools** ribbon appear. Tables are also one of the elements that can control text flow. The default is for a table to be treated like a paragraph inserted into the text stream. You can however adjust table properties to anchor the table and have the text flow around it in a manner similar to how text can flow around graphic elements. Chapter 6 discusses tables more fully.

Figures, Graphics, Text Boxes, and Equations

This family of elements includes images (as graphic files), built-in graphics such as clip art, shapes, "smart art", and text boxes. Including these elements together would probably cause a serious desk top publishing person to head into a tail spin, but we're bunching them together due to the fact that they all share similar attributes regarding how they are placed within a document, and in particular how text can flow around the element. Each inserted element is contained within a box which can flow with the text or be anchored to a location on the page. In the majority of cases, text flow can be highly customized to create sophisticated ragged edges that help to incorporate the graphic element with the text.

Another common feature of these elements is the ability to create a **Caption**. Captions are special fields that automatically keep track of sequential numbering for elements such as figures or tables. You can create custom captions as well—for example to caption *Exhibits*. Captions, both the built-in and custom ones, may then be included in a reference table. Thus it is possible to create a Table of Figures, Table of Exhibits, etc.

Equations are similar to figures and graphics in that they are either embedded in the text stream or anchored so text flows around the element. Equations also have a built-in caption type, so like the previous elements, it is easy to caption equations and to create a table of equations. Equations differ however in that they are usually created from within Microsoft Word using the **Equation Editor**.

Cross References

A cross reference, like the caption element just discussed, consists of a special embedded field that references some other location within a document. Typical examples include such phrases as "this is discussed in greater detail beginning on page 34", or "See Chapter 8". A cross reference may be made to a number of document objects, including headings (using the built-in *Heading* styles), bookmarks, numbered items, foot and end notes, and any of the items that are associated with captions. The cross reference text may include the text of the referenced item or the page number where the item is located. References automatically update as pages are inserted or deleted, or as the referenced text changes. Cross references are discussed in Chapter 8.

Table of Contents

In Microsoft Word, a Table of Contents is also an embedded field and therefore shares some attributes with captions and cross references. A table of contents is a more sophisticated element. This is reflected in the degree of customization you can create. In general, a table of contents pulls the entries and their page numbers from elements in the document marked to particular styles. The default behavior is to use the built-in *Heading* styles and the table organizes entries based on their heading level. For example if a document uses the *Heading 1* style to mark chapters and *Heading 2* style to mark divisions within a chapter, this organization is also reflected in the table of contents. The hierarchical organization, formatting, and which styles are used to tag table of contents entries is completely customizable.

The fact that you can create additional, specialty tables such as a table of figures or a table of exhibits was previously mentioned. You can also configure a table of contents so the figures, exhibits, and other captioned items appear within the greater structure of a single table. In all cases, a table of contents, like the other embedded field elements, update when you print or print preview the document, or when you manually force an update. Creating and managing a table of contents is discussed in Chapter 8.

Index

An index, like cross references and a table of contents, is also an embedded field. Unlike cross references and a table of contents, you must manually create the index entries for an index. This requirement reflects the fact that generating an index is a skill (some would elevate it to the status of an art) that requires careful preparation and thought. Word supports the use of *concordance files* to assist in the automatic generation of an index, although the creation of the concordance file still requires skill and is a manual process. The process of marking text for inclusion into an index, creating a concordance file, and managing indices is discussed in Chapter 8.

Glossaries and Appendices

The last class of elements, Glossaries and Appendices, does not represent a special type of Microsoft Word element. Rather structures such as a glossary, an appendix, an exhibit, or any other specialized section of a document is really just that—a specialized section of a document. These typically will be contained within dedicated sections, especially if the text within a header or footer is different. Example: using the text *Appendix A: Glossary of Terms* within the footer. Because these elements are usually associated with Sections, they will be covered in Chapter 4.

Chapter 3 | Working with Styles

Styles are predefined formatting attributes which can be applied to characters, paragraphs, or both elements. Using styles removes the tedium of manually applying formatting in a document, and when used appropriately, gives the editor great flexibility in making wholesale changes to the structure and appearance of a document. Recent versions of Microsoft Word ship with a large array of built-in styles, grouped as *Quick Sets* of styles. *Themes*, also relatively new to Microsoft Word, enforce color and font schemes across a Style Quick Set. You can create your own styles, define new Style Quick Sets, and modify existing styles.

Style Quick Sets are stored as a document *template*. When you create your own styles or modify existing ones you can choose to isolate the style to the current document or make the change to the document's underlying template.

Why Use Styles?

There are a number of reasons to use styles. At a trivial level, styles simply save you time when generating a document. Even for a relatively simple document that contains only body text and one or two heading styles, you save time by applying a style rather than selecting numerous format properties from the **Font** or **Paragraph** groups or from their respective dialog boxes.

There are a number of non-trivial reasons to use styles and all of them focus on the larger issues of structure and management of a complex document. First, when you consistently apply a style to the paragraphs in a complex document, any changes you wish to apply to those paragraphs—for example, to increase the spacing after each paragraph or to adjust the left margin—are made only once by modifying the style definition. The instant the modification is applied all paragraphs in that style automatically update. For people who aren't used to working with styles it is a simply a matter of how you view a complex document. Is the document a series of hundreds of paragraphs, all stitched together in a text stream, or it is a set of consistent containers, all structurally identical and recognized as paragraphs and identified by a style, that each contains one unit of thought within the larger text stream? If the latter concept makes sense you either already use styles or you're primed and ready to begin.

The second reason for using styles again looks at the larger structure of a complex document. When you consistently apply certain styles to the headings and subheading within a document, you are preparing the document for easy inclusion of a table of contents. The document is ready for cross references as well. Styles provide hooking points for other elements, mainly those that cross reference, to make the document useable by the end reader. Manually creating cross references or building a table of contents is a tedious nightmare. The instant an additional page is added to the middle of a document with manual referencing the references become obsolete and have to be done over again.

The third reason styles are useful is to enforce continuity of formatting across multiple documents. Many organizations create and distribute in house defined styles which are used to format the organization's documents. Very large organizations may manage whole families of styles so the groups that generate policy documents retain a related set of formatting styles for their needs which are very different from the groups that create press releases or publicity-related documents. Even if you are a single author but plan on creating a series of books, using styles ensures that the look and feel of your creative output is consistent between documents.

These three arguments focus on the use of paragraph styles, but character styles also have their place. A character style does not offer a hook to feed into cross reference elements, but the ability to consistently apply a set of font attributes to create text with emphasis or special meaning is still a time saving activity. Like paragraph styles, if you modify a character style all characters in the document based on that style are immediately updated.

Types of Styles

There are 5 style types that Word recognizes, but two of them: list and table styles, are so different from the older text and paragraph styles that we'll deal with them toward the end of this chapter. For general text flow Word recognizes three types of styles:

- **Character Styles** are denoted in most lists and dialog boxes with a lowercase letter a (**a**). Styles of this type only apply to characters and not paragraphs and thus only include the various attributes associated with fonts. Thus font name, size, text color, spacing, and attributes such as bold or italic text are all part of the specification for a character style.

- **Paragraph Styles** appear with a paragraph symbol (¶) in lists and dialog boxes. They include the attributes of a character style and extend those attributes to include all of those associated with paragraphs. Any attributes available from the **Paragraph** dialog box can be applied to a paragraph style, including shading, borders, and tabs.

- **Linked Styles** are identified by combining the paragraph and character style symbols (¶ a) and are relatively new to Word. A linked style is basically a paragraph style that is applied in a context-sensitive manner. If you highlight text and apply a linked style, only the character attributes of the style are applied and then only to the selected text. If the insertion point is in a paragraph and no text is selected, applying a linked style applies the paragraph style. If the paragraph is highlighted, both character and paragraph attributes are applied.

Styles are stored either in a template or in the current document. The built-in styles which ship with Microsoft Word are located in the **Normal.dotx** template and automatically migrate to any new template you create that is based on Normal.dotx. Whenever you create a new style or modify an existing one and the current document is based on **Normal.dotx**, if you permit Word to update the underlying template, then all documents based on **Normal.dotx** are also updated.

When you create a new style or modify an existing one you may choose to isolate the new or modified style to the current document or cascade the style down to the document's template. When you choose to save the new or modified style to the underlying template any document based on that template is also modified. This is true for both the **Normal.dotx** template and any custom template you work with. If you create custom templates, for example to unify the look and appearance of a series of documents you create and/or work with, and the current document is based on that template, you can choose to cascade the new or updated style to that template.

Using Styles

Working with styles can get a bit daunting, in part because Microsoft has added so many seemingly unrelated groups, dialog boxes, and panes that manage styles. One of these, the **Apply Styles** dialog box was introduced on page 11. It and the remaining style-related controls will be discussed in this section.

It was mentioned in the Introduction (page 12) that we will not survey the myriad of built-in styles and themes in this book. It is the opinion of the author that knowing how to create and modify styles is a far more powerful skill set and it removes you from the dependence on one company's predefined set of styles, regardless of how many built-in styles now appear with Microsoft Word.

Style Management Tools

Before we discuss using or managing styles, it would be useful to inventory the style tools Word offers.

The Styles Group

This tool is always visible when the **Home** tab is selected. It displays the **Style Quick Gallery**, the **Change Styles** control, and a **Dialog Expander** that opens the **Styles Pane**.

The **Style Quick Gallery** lists a set of styles that are related by being grouped into a **Style Set**. You can add or remove styles from this gallery. An example of the **Style Quick Gallery** is illustrated below.

In the lower right corner of the **Style Quick Gallery** is a short scroll bar. Choosing it opens a menu with the following options:

Style Quick Gallery Options

Option	Description
Save Selection as a New Quick Style (2007) / Create a Style (2010/2013)	Saves the selected text to a new Quick Style. During this process, if you choose **Modify..** the **Modify Style** dialog box will appear, otherwise the current attributes are saved to a style you name.
Clear Formatting	Applies the **Normal** style to the selected text.
Apply Styles	Opens the **Apply Styles** dialog box.

Change Styles (2007)

To the far right of the **Style Quick Gallery** is the **Change Styles** control. Selecting it opens a drop down menu with the following options:

Change Styles Options (2007)

Option	Description
Style Set...	Provides a list of the available style sets, or lets you reset the current style set either using **Normal.dotx** (reset document quick styles) or to the custom template (if using - in this case the menu command is Reset to Quick Styles from Template). You can also save the current style gallery to a new Style Set. Saving a Quick Style Set loads the styles in a document template in a folder named *QuickStyles*.
Colors...	Pick a color theme or create your own theme.
Font...	Change fonts or create a new theme font (you can specify heading and body fonts only).
Set as Default	Sets the current Style Set and Theme as the default and stores this information in **Normal.dotx**

Change Styles Equivalents in 2010/2013

For later versions of Microsoft Word, the **Change Styles** related functions have been moved to the new **Design** tab.

Change Styles Options (2010/2013)

Option	Description
Style Sets	The Word 2007 equivalent of style sets now appears in the **Document Formatting** group on the **Design** tab. Select from a gallery of predefined styles or choose the **Down Arrow** associated with the **Style Set Gallery** and select **Save as a new style set...**
Colors...	Pick a color theme or create your own theme. In 2010 and 2013, this is an individual command located in the **Document Formatting** group on the **Design** tab.
Font...	Change fonts or create a new theme font (you specify heading and body fonts only). This control is now located next to the **Colors** control (see above).
Set as Default	Sets the current Style Set and Theme as the default and stores this information in **Normal.dotx** This control is now located in the **Document Formatting** group on the **Design** tab.

The Styles Pane

This facility lists every available style as well as provides access to additional style tools. Its default behavior is to appear as a docked pane, but by dragging the pane title bar you can move it to another docked location (for example, to the left of the document) or cause it to appear as an always-on-top floating dialog box.

How to Open the Styles Pane

Step 1.   From the **Styles** group on the **Home** tab, choose the **Dialog Expander**. Alternatively, press *Alt Ctrl Shift S*. The **Styles Pane** will appear similar to the following:

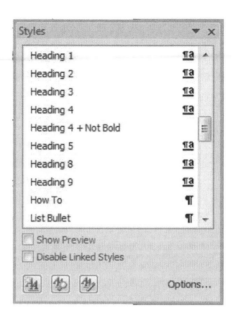

Style Pane Options

Option	Description
Style List	Used to apply the style; select all elements formatted in a style; remove all formatting based on a style; modify or remove a style.
Show Preview	Toggles the Style List to display the style name formatted in that style versus simply displaying style names as plain text.
Disable Linked Styles	When enabled, prevents you from using a linked style (they will still appear). For example, when enabled applying a paragraph style to selected text within a paragraph will apply the paragraph style to the entire paragraph. When disabled, only the character attributes of the paragraph style would be applied and only to the selected text.
New Style	Opens the **Create New Style** dialog box.
Style Inspector	Opens the **Style Inspector** dialog box.
Manage Styles	Opens the **Manage Style** dialog box. This facility is discussed beginning on page 39.
Options	Controls which styles (by type, by usage, or by parent document) are displayed in the **Styles Pane**.

The Style Inspector

This dialog is a short version of the **Styles Pane** with the exception that you cannot change styles using this tool. The only functional option is to remove the current style which has the effect of applying the **Normal** style.

How to Open the Style Inspector

Step 1.   If not visible, open the **Styles Pane** using the previous procedure as a guide.

Step 2.   At the bottom of the **Style Pane**, locate and select the **Style Inspector** button. The **Style Inspector** will appear similar to the following illustration:

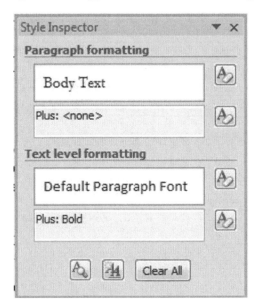

The Apply Styles Dialog Box

There are moments when Microsoft does things that completely boggle the mind. Burying the **Apply Styles** dialog is such a moment. In early versions of Microsoft Word this tool occupied the lofty position of far left on the old **Formatting** toolbar. Since Word 2007 it is only available for those of us who remember the keyboard shortcut to activate the tool. The utility in working with this tool from the author's perspective is that you can apply styles without leaving the keyboard, whereas every other method requires that you grab the mouse and start clicking.

How to Open the Apply Styles Dialog Box

The default for this dialog box is to open as an always-on-top dialog but it can be dragged to a docked location.

Step 1.   From the keyboard, press the ***Ctrl Shift S*** key combination. The **Apply Styles** dialog box will appear as follows:

Apply Styles Options

Option	Description
Style name	Lists the current style and can be used to apply a different style. When this combo box has the focus (which it does whenever the ***Ctrl Shift S*** key combination is issued) you can type out the name of a style and the list will auto scroll to the style name. Pressing ***Enter*** will apply the style.
Reapply	Reapplies the current style at the current cursor location or selection in the document. This is useful if you muck up a style and need to clean things up.
Modify	Opens the **Modify Style** dialog box. This tool is discussed on page 36.
Styles	Toggles the display of the **Styles Pane**.
AutoComplete style names	When enabled, allows the **Style Name** combo box to auto complete the style name as you type.

Applying a Style

Styles are applied to characters or paragraphs, either by first selecting the style and creating the text, or by highlighting existing text or paragraphs and applying the style. The character style is extended if you position the insertion point within or at the end of the character stream with the applied style and add more text. Generally, paragraph styles are extended to the next paragraph by simply pressing ***Enter*** to end one paragraph and begin a new one. Note however that a paragraph style can be defined such that once the initial paragraph has been created, the following paragraph is automatically formatted in another style. This is very useful when working with paragraph styles intended to format headings. After the heading has been created the following paragraph is automatically created in some style more appropriate for body text. This will be discussed in more detail when explaining how to create a style.

The **Format Painter** is also used to transfer styles, as will be discussed shortly.

How to Apply a Style

When you select a character style, only text characters adopt the new style. Applying a paragraph style will affect the current paragraph or currently selected paragraphs. If you have not disabled linked styles, applying a linked style depends upon what is presently selected. If text is selected then the linked style character attributes are applied. If the insertion point is in a paragraph (nothing is selected) or the paragraph mark is selected the paragraph and character styles are applied.

The following table highlights applying a style depending upon which tool you use.

Tool	Method
Quick Style	Position the insertion point in the desired location or select the desired text and/or paragraph, then click on the desired style.
Styles Pane	Follow the selection procedure as outlined above, then select the desired style from the list of styles.
Apply Styles	Use *Ctrl Shift S* to open or activate the **Style Name** drop down box. Begin typing the name of the style and once displayed, press *Enter*.
Keyboard Shortcut	If you have customized the keyboard to activate a style, type the key combination assigned to that style. Customizing the keyboard is discussed below.

How to Assign a Style to a Keyboard Shortcut

When you assign a custom keyboard shortcut to activate a style, the assignment is stored either with the document or with the document's template. In the latter case the keyboard shortcut is available to any document based on that template.

Step 1.   Select the **Office Button** (2007) or the **File** tab (2010/2013), and from the menu that appears, choose **Word Options**.

Step 2.   On the **Word Options** dialog, choose **Customize**.

Step 3. In the **Keyboard Shortcuts** area, choose **Keyboard**. The **Customize Keyboard** dialog box will appear similar to the following:

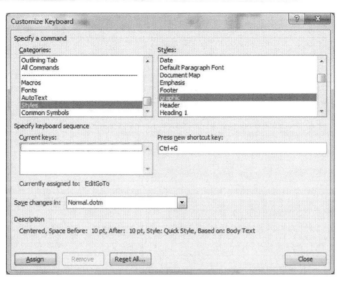

Step 4. In the **Categories** area, select **Styles**, then from the **Styles** area, select the desired style for the shortcut.

Step 5. If any current shortcuts exist for this style, they will appear in the **Current Keys** area. If you do not need to assign an additional shortcut choose **Close**. This would end this procedure.

Step 6. Activate the **Press new shortcut key** text box and enter the desired keyboard shortcut. For example, in the illustration above the key combination *Ctrl G* was entered. If this key combination is already assigned, its purpose will appear in the **Currently assigned to** area.

Step 7. If there is a current assignment for your proposed keyboard shortcut and you wish to preserve the original shortcut, clear the text in the **Press new shortcut key** area and try another combination. If there are no assignments for your proposed key combination, or if you wish to reassign the current assignment continue with this procedure.

Step 8. Use the **Save changes in** control to save the assignment to the document's template or make the change only available to the current document (it will appear by its file name).

Step 9. Choose **Assign**, then select **Close** and return to the **Word Options** dialog box. Choose **OK** to close that dialog and return to Word.

Creating a Style

When you create a new style you choose whether to isolate the new style so it only applies to the current document, or to associate it with the document's template and therefore make it accessible to all documents that share the template. Styles may be migrated between documents and templates as well which is discussed on page 39.

You create a new style by working with the **Create Style** dialog box. There are three ways to begin:

- Use the **New Style** button located on the **Styles Pane** (in 2013 it is labeled **Create Style**).
- Select the **New Style** button from the **Style Inspector** dialog.
- For users of Word 2007 select existing text or a paragraph and right click. From the shortcut menu, choose **Styles**, then select **Save Selection as a New Quick Style**. When the **Create New Style from Formatting** dialog box appears, choose **Modify**. Note that this last step is essential if you wish to work with the **Create Style** dialog.

Regardless of the path chosen above, the **Create Style** dialog box will appear as illustrated. The various controls are explained in the following table.

Option	Description
Name	A descriptive name for the new style. This name will appear in any control that lists available styles.
Style type	Determines whether the new style is character, paragraph, or linked (default). The other options, *List* and *Table* will be discussed beginning on page 42.
Style based on	If you wish your new style to assume the attributes of an existing style, select that style from this list, otherwise select (*No Style*).
Style for following paragraph	For paragraph and linked styles, this controls which style will be applied to any paragraph created from the current paragraph (it does not force the next existing paragraph into a new style). For styles intended for body text the default is the name of the style you specified in the **Name** box. For styles intended to be headings or where you need the following paragraph to be different, choose the following paragraph style from the list.
Formatting	Displays two rows of common font (character) and paragraph attributes. If you are creating a character style the second row is disabled. For additional attributes use the **Format** button.
Preview Area	As format attributes are applied, the current section of the document appears and displays the current formatting.
Add to Quick Style list	Check to include this style in the **Quick Style List**.
Automatically update	If enabled and you make changes to a style, Word will update the style and automatically apply changes to all elements in the document using the style. Enable this feature with caution!
Only in this document / New documents based on this template	This is an either/or choice. The new style will either be located only in the current document or it will be stored in the template that the document is based on (for most users this is **Normal.dotx**).
Format	Opens a menu with additional formatting options: **Font** Opens the **Font** dialog box. **Paragraph** Opens the **Paragraph** dialog box. **Tabs** Set tab stops and tab attributes for a paragraph style. **Border** Control paragraph border attributes for paragraph style. **Language** Sets language-specific tools such as spelling and grammar. **Frame** Specifies frame settings for the paragraph style. **Numbering** Sets options for bulleted or numbered paragraph styles. **Shortcut Key** Jumps to the **Customize Keyboard** dialog box which was discussed on page 34.

How to Create a New Style

Use the previous illustration and table as a guide to this procedure.

Step 1.   Use one of the methods discussed on page 36 to open the **Create New Style** dialog box.

Step 2.   Name the style and specify whether it will be a character, paragraph or linked style.

Step 3.   If desired, base the new style on an existing style.

Step 4.   If creating a linked or a paragraph style such as a heading which requires a different style for the following paragraph, specify that style.

Step 5.   Use the controls in the **Formatting** area or select **Format** and select the desired category of style attributes.

Step 6.   Indicate whether the new style will be stored in the current document or in the template used to create the current document.

Step 7.   Choose **OK** to create the new style.

Modifying a Style

Any style—built in or custom—can be modified. Modifications involve the attributes associated with the style type so modifying a character style means making changes to the **Font** properties while changing a paragraph style offers a broader set of attributes that can be modified.

When you modify a style you must decide whether to modify the style only as it applies to the current document, or to cascade the change to the document's template. The latter option makes the modified style available to other documents that share the same template.

How to Modify a Style

You can begin this procedure by either using the **Styles Pane** or from the **Apply Styles** dialog box.

Step 1.   If using the **Style Pane**, position the mouse over the style to modify. When a drop down button appears, click on it and choose **Modify**.

If using the **Apply Styles** dialog, first select the style from the **Style Name** drop down box, then choose **Modify**.

Step 2.   The **Modify Style** dialog box will appear. It is identical to the **Create New Style** dialog box illustrated and discussed in the previous procedure. Make the modifications to the style as desired and select **OK** when done.

If modifying a built-in style or a style that is important to your work you may want to save the modified style to the current document first. Once you've worked with the modified style you can return to the **Modify Style** dialog and save the modified style to a template.

Managing Styles

Microsoft Word includes a tool, the **Manage Styles** dialog, which is helpful for performing certain management tasks. Of the tasks this dialog offers, perhaps the most useful is the ability to import or export styles between documents and templates. Another feature of this tool, the ability to restrict or permit usage of certain styles, will be discussed in Chapter 9 (Multiuser Documents).

One common style management technique is to move or copy styles between documents or templates. For example, you may create a style that is used to provide consistency to a logo. If you manage several custom templates in your work, copying this style to all work-related templates makes it accessible to any document based on any of your custom templates.

How to Import/Export Styles

Step 1.   If not visible, open the **Styles** pane (use the **Dialog Expander** on the **Styles** group or press *Alt Ctrl Shift S*).

Step 2.   At the bottom of the **Styles** pane, select **Manage Styles**. The **Manage Styles** dialog will appear:

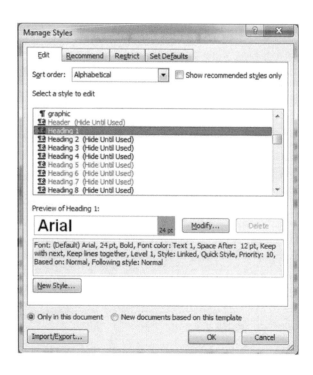

Tab/Control	Description
Edit	A convenient location for modifying existing styles or creating new styles.
Recommend	Controls the order in which styles appear as *Recommended Styles*.
Restrict	Permits the enabling/disabling of styles - used when you distribute a document for comment/editing. Discussed in Chapter 9.
Set Defaults	Set default attributes for specific fonts.
Import/Export	Opens the **Organizer** which is used to move styles between documents or templates.

Step 3.   Choose **Import/Export**. The **Organizer** will appear similar to the following:

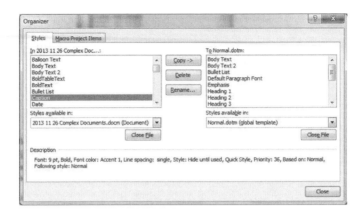

The controls on the left-hand side of the **Styles** tab generally relate to the current document, while the right-hand controls relate to the underlying template. The source and destination files can be changed by use of the **Close File** button.

Option	Description
In / To *filename*	Names the current document. This can change by using the **Close File** command. The prefix *In* and *To* may also toggle depending upon which style window is used to select a style to move.
Styles available in	Lists the styles available in the document named above the list window. Also lists the document serving as the source for the style list.
Close File	Closes the document and toggles to an **Open File** command. Use this to choose another document or template to act as a source or target to move styles.
Copy	Copies the selected file to the other document. The direction of the copy operation depends upon whether a style was selected from the left or right side of the dialog box.
Delete	Deletes the selected style.
Rename	Renames the selected style. This is useful if you are importing a style into a document that contains a style of the same name.

Step 4.   Use the previous table as a guide to direct how styles are exported or imported. If the source or target document isn't available, choose **Close File**, then **Open File** and select another document or template.

Step 5.   Select **Close** when done.

To *move* a style first export (or import) it, then delete the style from the source document.

Special Styles

Relatively new to the style scene are list and table styles. In both cases, Microsoft Word has attempted to create styles that format fairly complex objects. Lists are specialized paragraphs that can contain highly ordered indentation levels. Tables are unique structures—essentially cellular in their organization—that contain rows and columns with each row, column, or intersecting cell being differentiable from its neighbor. Implementation of the list style is generally straightforward as it is essentially a special case of the paragraph style. Table styles are a unique case. We will soon see that they have issues and limitations and yet still offer some general applicability for complex documents.

List Styles—A Primer

A numbered or bulleted list in Microsoft Word is really a series of paragraphs bound together by a common list style. For simple numbered or bulleted lists, every list item is in the same style and all share the same *Outline Level*. For numbered lists, the fact that each paragraph starts with an incremented number is immaterial—the list style is still the same between items, as is the outline level.

When you create a multi-level list you add a layer of complexity. Consider the following simple example of a multilevel list with three outline levels:

Multilevel·List·Demo¶
¶
1)→ This·is·list·item·one·-·level·one¶
    a)→ Sub·item·a·-·level·two¶
    b)→ Sub·item·b·-·level·two¶
       i)→ Sub·item·i·-·level·three¶
      ii)→ Sub·item·ii·-·level·three¶
    c)→ Sub·item·c·-·level·two¶
2)→ List·item·two·-·level·one¶

The text illustrated above was created using one of Word's built-in list styles. If you inspect any paragraph however, the style listed is called **List Paragraph**. If you open the **Reveal Formatting** pane and probe the **Bullets and Numbering** section, each **Outline Level** will be indicated, but every paragraph is in the same style, even though the numbering scheme (here using Arabic numerals, then lowercase letters, then small Roman numerals) is different, as is the indentation level. So a list style is really a related family of paragraph styles, each identified by its outline level.

One odd feature of list styles is that Word will prevent you from selecting a single item in a list and specifying paragraph attributes just for that item. If you wish to set all items within outline level 2 apart by increasing paragraph spacing before and after you must select *all* items at that level and then specify the spacing.

Working with Simple List Styles

You cannot modify existing bullet or numbered lists but you can create custom ones. Any new list style you create can be added to the **Bullet Library** or the **Numbering Library** and any item in either library may be removed. If you are working with a simple bullet or numbered list and decide to begin indenting (which has the effect of creating paragraphs in outline levels greater than level 1), Word will assign a predetermined bullet or number style to the various outline levels you use. For full control over the appearance of outline levels beyond level 1, consider creating a custom multilevel list (discussed below).

How to Create a New Bullet Style

Step 1.   Position the insertion point at the location in your document where you wish to begin a new bullet list.

Step 2.   Select the drop down arrow associated with the **Bullets** button located within the **Paragraph** group on the **Home** tab.

Step 3.   Choose **Define New Bullet….** The **Define New Bullet** dialog box will appear similar to the following:

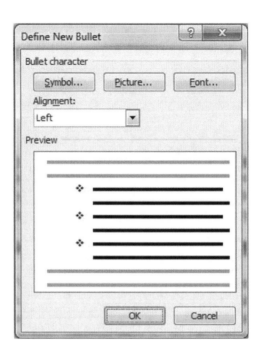

Option	Description
Symbol	Opens the **Symbol** dialog box. This dialog will default to a symbol font, although all characters and symbols from all fonts installed on your computer are available.
Picture	Opens the **Picture Gallery** dialog box. This tool will search for installed icons and pictures from the Microsoft Office or allow you to import an image.
Font	Make adjustments to font attributes (only if using a symbol). Font size, color, and attributes such as bold or italic may be selected.
Alignment	Within a narrow region where the bullet will appear, you can set alignment to the left, center, or right of this region.

Step 4.   Make the desired selections to create a new custom bullet style and choose **OK**. The new bullet style will be applied to the current cursor location.

Removing a Custom Bullet Style

Step 1.   Select the drop down arrow associated with the **Bullets** button located within the **Paragraph** group on the **Home** tab.

Step 2.   Locate the desired bullet style from within the **Bullet Library** area and right-click on it.

Step 3.   From the shortcut menu, choose **Remove**.

Any existing bullet lists using the former style are *not* affected. You will need to step through the document and reapply another bullet style where necessary.

Working with Multi-Level List Styles

Multi-level lists contain two or more outline levels whereas the items in a simple list are all at the same outline level. The following illustration is an example of a multi-level list that displays three outline levels:

Multilevel List Demo¶
¶
1)→ This is list item one - level one¶
   a)→ Sub item a - level two¶
   b)→ Sub item b - level two¶
     i)→ Sub item i - level three¶
     ii)→ Sub item ii - level three¶
   c)→ Sub item c - level two¶
2)→ List item two - level one¶

In the example, the top-most level (Word refers to this level simply as *Level 1*) use Arabic numerals (1, 2, 3, etc.) to identify items at the level 1 outline level. Items at outline level 2 are identified with lowercase letters (a, b, c, etc.) while items in outline level three use lowercase Roman numerals (i, ii, iii, etc.).

Of the various stylistic attributes that you can apply to a multi-level list, the most common are the format used to denote members of a particular outline level and the amount of indentation to apply to each. Thus, when you create or modify a multi-level list you manipulate attributes of the various outline levels. Word supports up to 9 outline levels, although in practice most authors use far fewer.

How to Create a New Multi-level List Style

The techniques illustrated here apply to modifying an existing multi-level list as well.

Step 1.   From the **Paragraph Group** on the **Home** tab, choose **Multilevel List**, then select **Define New List Style**. The **Define New List Style** dialog box will appear similar to the following:

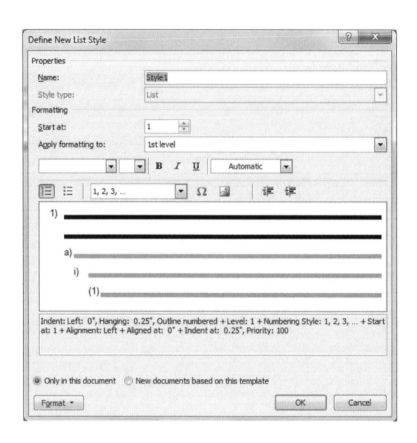

Option	Description
Name	Define a name for the list style. Note that the **Style Type** is disabled as you are creating a list style.
Start at	The number or letter which should start the selected list level. This is almost always *1, A, a, i,* etc.
Apply formatting to	Use to specify the list level you wish to define. Any formatting change you make will apply to the currently-displayed list level. At any point you can select another list level and continue specifying format attributes to that level.
Only in this document	Indicates whether to store the new list style only in the current document or in the template that the current document is based on. Generally the latter choice would store the style in *normal.dot*
Format	Provides access to the **Font**, **Numbering**, and **Shortcut Key** dialog boxes.

Step 2.   If defining a new style, ensure that the **Apply formatting to** control is set to *1st level*, otherwise, use this control to select the desired outline level to modify.

Step 3.   Make formatting adjustments to the selected outline level. The first row of controls specify font attributes which will apply to the lettering or numbering scheme (if applicable). The second row of controls sets **Numbering** or **Bullet** styles, the style of numbering or bullets to use as well as controls to set a specific symbol or picture for a bullet style. For each outline level you can switch between numbering and bullet styles.

Step 4.   If additional font or numbering attributes are desired, select the **Font** or **Numbering** dialog from the **Format** command button. Note that these settings *only* affect the style of the numbered items and not any text associated with each outline level.

Step 5.   If you desire to specify or modify additional outline levels, return to the **Apply formatting to** control, choose the next outline level and repeat Steps 3 and 4.

Step 6.   Choose **OK** when done.

 When working with your custom multilevel list style the various dialog boxes that display styles will not show your custom multilevel list style. To modify a custom list style, select the style from the list style gallery (**Multilevel List** control in the **Paragraph** group on the **Home** tab) by right-clicking on it, then select **Modify**.

 When the insertion point is within a custom list style the actual style displayed in the **Apply Styles** or **Style Inspector** dialogs will be *List Paragraph*. Only the **Reveal Formatting** pane will identify your custom style.

 Another option from the **Multilevel List** command is **Define New Multilevel List**. This command is used to create a list style that may be quickly applied but not modified. It is useful when you need a custom multilevel list applied in a single document.

Removing a Multi-Level List Style

Step 1.   If not visible, open the **Styles** pane by choosing the **Dialog Expander** button on the **Styles** group of the **Home** tab (alternatively, press *Alt Ctrl Shift S*).

Step 2.   On the **Styles** pane, choose the **Manage Styles** button.

Step 3.   Ensure that the **Sort Order** control on the **Manage Styles** dialog is set to *Alphabetical*, then scroll through the list of styles to locate the desired custom list style.

Step 4.   Select the desired style and choose **Delete**. Close the dialog box.

Table Styles

Table styles are similar to list styles in that they only apply to a specific object in a document —in this case to the formatting of a table. This type of style definition sets such attributes as background color and fill, boarding line formats and font attributes. Because tables are fairly complex objects (refer to Chapter 6 for details), you may specify different format attributes for such entities as the first (heading) or last (totals) row of a table, the first or last column within a table, odd or even numbered rows, etc.

As with list styles, if you wish to create a new table style or modify an existing one, use that style consistently throughout a document.

How to Apply a Table Style

Step 1.   Insert a new table into a document or select an existing table.

Step 2.   Select a predefined table style from the list of **Table Styles** on the **Design | Table Tools** tab. You may need to scroll through the gallery to view all available styles.

How to Create a Table Style

Ensure that the insertion point is within an existing table before following this procedure.

Step 1.   From the **Table Styles** group on the **Design | Table Tools** tab, select **More** (the down arrow associated with the gallery scroll bar), then choose **New Table Style…** The **New Table Style** dialog box will appear similar to the following:

Option	Description
Properties	These controls let you name the new style, determine the style type, and if desired, choose an existing style to serve as a template for the new style.
Apply formatting to..	Selects the scope for any formatting options you choose. The following table explains this control.
Formatting	These controls set border line style, border line weight, border line color, border pattern, background color, cell text alignment, and font attributes. As you make selections the table preview area updates.
Format	Provides access to the **Font**, **Paragraph**, **Borders and Shading**, **Banding**, and **Table Properties** dialog boxes. Each of these provides additional formatting selections.

The attributes that you select using this dialog box are applied to the table area displayed in the **Apply formatting to** drop down box. The options are as follows:

Option	Description
Whole table	Formatting is applied to the entire table.
Header/Total Row	Applies formatting only to the Header or Total Row. These rows are specifically defined by choosing **Header Row** and/or **Total Row** from the **Table Style Options** group on the **Design	Table Tools** tab. If a **Header** and/or **Total** row isn't defined in the current table, these formatting attributes will not be applied.
First/Last Column	As above. The **First** and **Last Column** must be selected using the **Table Style Options** group to define these structures in a table.
Odd/Even banded Rows	Defines formatting for the odd or even-numbered rows in a table. By default a band is a single row. To define 2 or more rows as being part of a band, use the **Band** option available from the **Format** button on the **Create New Style** dialog box.
Odd/Even banded Columns	As above except it applies to columns.
Top/Left, Top/Right, Bottom/Left, Bottom/Right Cell	Set formatting attributes for the upper right, upper left, lower right, and/or lower left-most cell in the table.

Step 2.   Type a name for the new style and, if desired, select an existing table style to serve as a template for your new style.

Step 3.   Ensure that the desired part of the table you wish to style is selected in the **Apply formatting to** drop down box.

Step 4.   Use the formatting controls on the dialog box to make the desired selections. For more detailed options, select the appropriate dialog box from the **Format** drop down box.

Step 5.   Choose **OK** to save the new style.

Any table styles you create will be listed in the **Custom** area of the **Table Styles** gallery as well as in the **Apply Styles** dialog box. They will not be listed in the **Styles** dialog box.

How to Modify a Table Style

Ideally the insertion point should be within a table based on the style you wish to modify. The note box following this procedure outlines how to modify a table style when the insertion point is not within a table based on the style to modify.

Step 1.   In the **Table Styles** group on the **Design | Table Tools** tab, select the down arrow to open the style gallery.

Step 2.   In the **Custom** area, right-click on the desired style and choose **Modify...** from the short cut menu. The **Modify Style** dialog box will appear similar to the following:

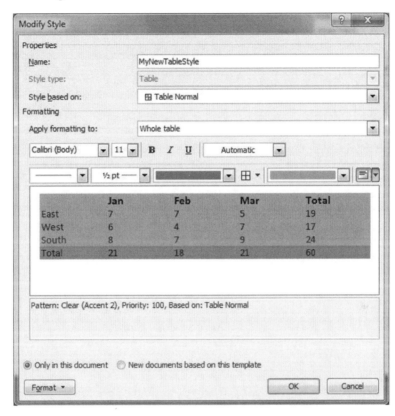

Step 3.   Ensure that the desired table object (for example, whole table or total row) is selected in the **Apply formatting to** drop down box.

Step 4.   Make the desired formatting changes.

Step 5.   If you wish to modify other portions of the table style, select the next table area to modify from the **Apply formatting to** drop down box, then repeat Step 4.

Step 6.   Choose **OK** when done.

To modify a table style without being in a table, open the **Apply Styles** dialog box by using the *Ctrl Shift S* keystroke combination. Locate the desired style in the **Style Name** drop down box, then choose **Modify**. Proceed beginning with Step 3 in the previous procedure.

How to Delete a Custom Table Style

Step 1.   In the **Table Styles** group on the **Design | Table Tools** tab, select the down arrow to open the style gallery.

Step 2.   In the **Custom** area, right-click on the desired style and choose **Delete Table Style**.

Chapter 4 | Working with Sections

Chapter 2 discussed the three levels of organization in a Microsoft Word document—characters, paragraphs, and sections. As was discussed, sections are the highest-level of organization in a document. Styles are used to manage pages that share some attribute such as a common page orientation, common header or footer style, or contain columns of text.

Whenever you need to change an attribute such as page margins, paper source (for printing), page orientation, or the style of a header or footer, you generally implement the change by inserting a *section break* to create a new section. In a manner similar to the way that new characters inherit the character attributes while you type, and a new paragraph inherits the paragraph attributes from the previous paragraph, when you insert a new section via a section break the default is for the new section to inherit the attributes of the previous section. Once the focus is in the newly-created section you then manipulate the desired section attributes. Many of these are managed via the **Page Setup** group located on the **Page Layout** tab.

It is common for complex documents that contain chapters to utilize a scheme where the headers and/or footers for each chapter are different. Using sections to achieve this goal is a common practice. Indeed, the print version of this book was created in Microsoft Word and every chapter maps to a separate section in order to achieve footers that present page number *and* chapter title.

About Sections

Sections generally map to the attributes we think of as being related to a page, such as margins and page orientation. In character-based word processors such as WordPerfect, the author may manipulate page attributes (such as the content of a page footer or the orientation of a single page) without having to resort to extra steps. This type of manipulation isn't available in Microsoft Word. For whatever reason, Microsoft decided to wrap attributes that we think of as belonging to a single page into a larger structure we now refer to as a section. Sections can cause a casual user of Microsoft Word problems, and indeed if the user is migrating from WordPerfect, sections can be outright bizarre. The more you know about sections and the logic behind their use the better prepared you'll be when you encounter section-related problems.

To begin, review the section attributes first presented in the table on page 23. With the exception of some types of headers and footers, anytime you need to change any of the attributes listed in that table, you'll need to create a section break. In the case of headers and footers, if you wish to prevent a header or footer from appearing on the first page within a section, or you need to use different headers or footers for odd and even-numbered pages, those attributes are already built in to the section. However, if you intend to create headers and/or footers which change between chapters (as the footers do in this book), you must create separate sections that will contain the custom headers or footers associated with chapters, appendices, or whatever level of organization your document requires.

Perhaps the single issue surrounding sections that can drive even a seasoned user of Microsoft Word crazy is creating different headers and footers. This is usually due to a pesky little property named *Same as Previous* that is applied by default when you create two or more sections in a document. We'll tackle this little beast head on when we discuss working with headers and footers later in this Chapter.

When working with a document that contains more than one section, the number of the current section is displayed in the status bar, which appears in the lower left of the Word screen. An example is illustrated below:

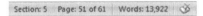

 When working with a document that contains multiple sections, it is a good idea to use the status bar as a way to monitor which section you are in (meaning where the insertion point is currently located). This is especially true if you wish to work with **Show/Hide** disabled.

 The **Object Browser** (2007/2010), discussed on page 7, offers the ability to quickly step between sections in a document. Remarkably, the **Browse by section** option is missing in Word 2013. See the discussion on page 218.

Inserting Sections

Sections are inserted using the **Page Setup** group on the **Page Layout** tab. There are 4 types of section breaks as discussed in the following table.

Section Breaks

Type	Description
Next Page	Inserts a new page or continues text on the next page (if the break is placed within text). In either case, the new page is a member of a new section.
Continuous	Creates a new section but on the current page. The most common use for this type of section break is to establish two or more columns in the text stream, or whenever the number of columns changes. Generally, *continuous* section breaks are paired to contain a region where columns are used in a document.
Even Page	This type of section break will dynamically add or remove a blank page to ensure that the first page of the next section begins on an even-numbered page.
Odd Page	As above, except the new section begins on an odd-numbered page.

Section breaks are only visible when **Show/Hide** is enabled and you are working with the document in **Print Layout** view. The four types of section breaks appear similar to the following in a document:

Section Break (Next Page)

Section Break (Continuous)

Section Break (Even Page)

Section Break (Odd Page)

How to Insert a Section Break

Use the previous table as a guide to assist you in determining the appropriate type of section break.

Step 1.   Position the insertion point at the location in the document where a section break is required.

Step 2.   On the **Page Setup** group on the **Page Layout** tab, select the **Breaks** control.

Step 3.   In the **Section Breaks** area, select the desired section.

Warning: Under some circumstances a section break may appear truncated and may only display a short segment of the double line used to name the break type (for example if the break appears at the end of a sentence that spans nearly the page width). If a section break is forced to occupy a full page width (for example by placing a paragraph mark immediately above the section break, you can usually force the display of the full break.

Modifying Sections

You can delete a section break or change its type. Only delete a section break when you absolutely are no longer in need of its presence. To modify the type of section break, follow second procedure discussed below.

How to Delete a Section Break

Deleting a section break will force the text downstream of the deleted break to inherit the section properties of the previous section. For example, deleting a section break that had been used to create a page oriented to *Landscape* in section 2 while the pages in section 1 were oriented to *Portrait* will force the text in the former section 2 to adopt the *Portrait* page orientation.

Do not use this procedure when you wish to change the type of section break. That operation is discussed next.

Step 1.   Ensure that **Show/Hide** is enabled.

Step 2.   Position the insertion point immediately to the right (upstream) of the section break, then press the *Delete* key. In the following illustration the insertion point would be positioned between the paragraph mark and the right edge of the section break:

feugait ·nulla·facilisi. ·Lorem·ipsum·dolor·sit·amet, ·consectetuer·adipiscing·
elit, ·sed·diam·nonummy·nibh·euismod·tincidunt·ut·laoreet·dolore·magna·aliquam·
erat·volutpat. ·¶═══════════════════ Section Break (Next Page) ═══════════════════════

Pressing *Ctrl z* will immediately undo the delete action.

How to Change a Section Break

Using this procedure is preferred over deleting and re-inserting a section break when you need to change the break type. You must be *inside* the section you wish to change. This is unlike the procedure to delete a section break where you must be immediately upstream of the actual section break. If in doubt use the status bar (it displays the section number associated with the current insertion point location) to ensure that you are in the correct location in the document. Also recall that the **Object Browser** offers the ability to quickly jump to each section break within a document. When Word changes a section break type the original section break is not removed, it is converted to the desired new section break type.

Step 1.   Position the insertion point *inside* the section you wish to work with. For example, if you need to change the break type that establishes section 3, you position the insertion point somewhere inside section 3.

Step 2.   Move to the **Page Setup** group on the **Page Layout** tab and select the **Dialog Expander** (the small arrow located on the lower right corner of the group). The **Page Setup** dialog box will appear.

Step 3.   Select the **Layout** tab.

Step 4.   Use the **Section Start** drop down box to change the section break.

Step 5.   Choose **OK** when done.

Page Attributes

This class of section-related attributes basically falls into two groups; page orientation and page margins. They relate to how the text stream will flow across a page. Paper size and paper source are real-world attributes that speak to the issue of physically printing a document. In both cases, if you need to change one of these attributes at some point in a document you must work with sections.

Page Orientation

Manipulating page orientation in a complex document is a fairly common task. Generally you need to switch from the more common portrait orientation to a landscape-oriented page when you must accommodate content that is too wide to fit the former orientation. When you change page orientation in a document that uses headers and/or footers, the location of the header or text does not rotate. How to work around this will be discussed in the discussion of headers and footers later in this Chapter.

We will discuss two procedures for changing page orientation. The first will cover how to add a landscape page at the bottom of a document and the other procedure will address how to conduct this operation *within* an existing multipage document.

How to Insert a Landscape Page at the End of a Document

Step 1.   Position the cursor at the point that reflects the end of the text stream in portrait orientation.

Step 2.   Select the **Page Layout** tab, then select **Breaks** from the **Page Setup** group.

Step 3.   Choose **Next Page** from the **Section Breaks** area. A next page section break will be inserted in your document.

Step 4.   Ensure that the insertion point is now within the newly created section. The default behavior is to insert the section break immediately upstream from the insertion point location and this should place the cursor within the new section. If not, use the status bar to ensure that you are in the target section.

Step 5.   Return to the **Page Setup** group and select **Orientation**, then choose **Landscape**. This procedure is summarized in the following illustration.

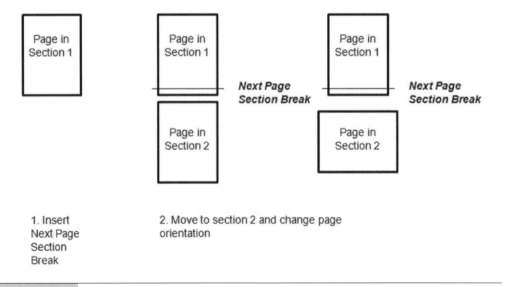

1. Insert Next Page Section Break

2. Move to section 2 and change page orientation

Any additional pages inserted or created within this new section will inherit the landscape orientation.

If you need to add additional pages beyond the landscape page (or pages), that change orientation back to portrait, continue with this procedure.

Step 6.   Position the insertion point at the end of the text stream for the landscape oriented section.

Step 7.   Repeat Steps 2 through 5, except select **Portrait** in Step 5.

How to Insert a Landscape Page within a Document

When you insert a landscape page or a series of pages within an existing document, it is a good idea to insert two next page section breaks and then set landscape orientation for the page or pages between these breaks. This is recommended because inserting only one section break before landscaping a page will force landscaping downward through the document (until another section break is encountered or the end of the document is reached). To prevent this from occurring inserting two section breaks isolates the portion of the document you wish to landscape.

Step 1.   Position the cursor at the point that reflects the end of the text stream in portrait orientation.

Step 2.   Select the **Page Layout** tab, then select **Breaks** from the **Page Setup** group.

Step 3.   Choose **Next Page** from the **Section Breaks** area. A next page section break will be inserted in your document.

Step 4.   Insert a few paragraph marks (use the ***Enter*** key), then repeat Steps 2 and 3. At this point you have isolated one section (between the newly inserted section breaks) from the rest of the document.

Step 5.   Position the insertion point between the new section breaks, then from the **Page Setup** group, select **Orientation**, then choose **Landscape**. This procedure is summarized in the following illustration.

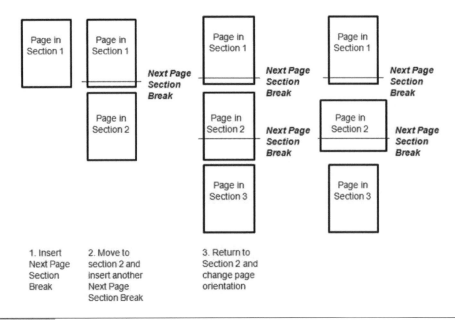

| 1. Insert Next Page Section Break | 2. Move to section 2 and insert another Next Page Section Break | 3. Return to Section 2 and change page orientation |

It is important to note that this method forces any downstream sections to be renumbered to the next highest value. For example, in the illustration above, content on page 2 is in section 2. That content is pushed downward, onto page 3 which is now renumbered section 3. Section 2 becomes the new, blank section just inserted in the document.

Page Margins

Creating a document that uses different page margins in two or more sections requires the use of section breaks. They are applied in a manner similar to either of the two procedures outlined in the previous section.

How to Create a Section with Different Page Margins

Step 1.   Follow either of the previous two procedures to establish a new section, or a new section within an existing document, then ensure that the insertion point is located within the new section.

Step 2.   From the **Page Setup** group on the **Page Layout** tab, choose **Margins**.

Step 3.   Select a predefined margin group from the gallery, or for more control over margins, select **Custom Margins**. The **Page Setup** dialog will appear as follows:

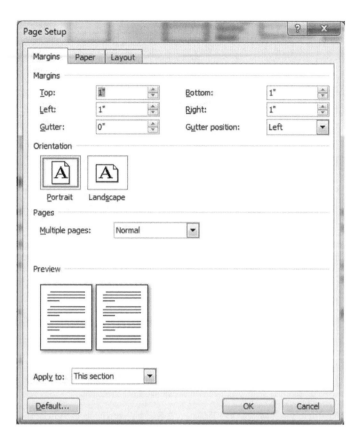

Step 4.   Use the controls in the **Margins** area to define your new page margins.

Step 5.   To isolate the new margin settings to the current section, ensure that the **Apply to** drop down box is set to *This section*. The other choices are *Whole document* or *This point forward*. The latter option sets the current margin settings for the current section and all sections downstream.

Step 6.   Choose **OK** when done.

How to Locally Override Page Margins

Another approach doesn't involve creating sections—rather, you modify the left and/or right paragraph indentation settings. The following illustration shows three paragraphs, all within the same section in a document. The middle paragraph has had its left indentation value set to *-0.5 inches*. Note that this forces the paragraph to run out to the left and beyond the page's left margin.

```
Lorem ipsum dolor sit amet, con
nibh euismod tincidunt ut laore
enim ad minim veniam, quis nost

Lobortis nisl ut aliquip ex ea commod
in hendrerit in vulputate velit esse
feugiat nulla facilisis at vero eros
blandit praesent luptatum zzril delen
facilisi.¶

¶
Ut wisi enim ad minim veniam, q
lobortis nisl ut aliquip ex ea
dolor in hendrerit in vulputate
```

Paper Attributes

The remaining page attributes, paper size and paper source, are associated with the real world and define the physical dimension of the paper the document will be printed on, as well as the paper tray the printer should use (assuming your printer supports this option). Two examples come to mind when considering these options. If you have a document that consists mainly of pages which are 8-1/2 x 11" (or A4 for European paper) and a landscape section of your document will require a larger format (for example, 8.5 x 14", or B5) then you would either create a separate section or modify an existing section to inform the printer of this change in paper size. This frequently also necessitates a change in paper source as many printers are equipped to handle two or more paper sizes. Another case where a separate paper source is required is in organizations that utilize a preprinted stock sheet for the first page with all other pages using plain paper.

How to Specify a Different Paper Size and/or Paper Source

Because these settings relate to the physical characteristics of the target printer, you must ensure that the printer is equipped to accept these settings. In particular, the options available for paper source are derived from the currently selected printer.

Step 1.   Use any of the techniques discussed under the section titled **Page Orientation** to either establish a new section or to move to the desired section.

Step 2.   From the **Page Setup** group on the **Page Layout** tab, choose **Size**.

Step 3.   Select a predefined paper size from the gallery, or for more control select **More paper sizes…** The **Page Setup** dialog will appear as:

Step 4.   To change paper size, select a predefined paper from the **Paper size** drop down
            box, or select **Custom** and enter the custom **Width** and **Height** settings. For
            clarity you may wish to include the appropriate measurement symbols such as ″
            or *cm*.

Step 5.   To change paper source for the current printer select the desired option in the
            First page and/or **Other pages** area. Note that the options available are
            derived from the currently selected printer.

Step 6.   Choose **OK** when done.

Headers and Footers

Headers and footers are another attribute of a section. In some cases a multipage document may
have one or more sections yet require that any headers and/or footers remain the same
throughout the document. This is the default behavior when you create a header or footer.

Within a section, Word offers four options for headers and footers as outlined in the following table.

Option	Description
Different first page	The first page of the section has a header and footer which is different from the remaining pages within the section. When enabled, this option creates a **First Page Header** and a **First Page Footer**.
Different Odd/Even	Within each section, two types of headers and footers exist: one type for odd and another type for even pages. If enabled, four objects are created for the section: **Even Page Header**, **Even Page Footer**, **Odd Page Header**, and **Odd Page Footer**.
All headers/footers the same	This is the default option if you create a header and/or a footer. Regardless of the number of sections in a document, a header or footer defined anywhere in the document becomes the header or footer for the entire document. When no other option has been specified and you enter Header/Footer design mode, there is a **Header** and a **Footer** object.
No headers or footers	This is the default option for all new documents. Word by default does not create a header or footer with content when you create a new document.

If you work with **Different Odd/Even** and the current section is only 1 page, one of the header/footer combinations will not be available until there is sufficient content to create an additional page (or you insert a page break). If **Different first page** is also enabled the section must contain at least 3 pages before all three types of headers and footers are visible.

These options are mediated through the **Layout** tab on the **Page Setup** dialog, or via the **Options** group when working in header and footer design mode.

When you create content for a header or footer, most of the objects such as paragraph borders and tables are available, as well as the standard font and paragraph attributes (such as font size or color and paragraph alignment). It's useful to think of the header and footer editing area as being small documents in their own right. In fact, when working in either a header or footer edit area, the body of the document appears gray and may not be edited. You must leave the header or footer editor to return to the document.

But before discussing any detailed issues concerning headers and footers, we need to understand the basics of page numbering. After all, placement of page numbers in a header or footer is the most common use of this area of a document.

Simple Page Numbering

The most common use of a running header or footer is to format page numbering for a document. Word has a gallery of predefined page number formats, although to fully understand page numbering you should know how to manually insert a page number, how to format page numbering, and how to specify how page numbering continues or starts anew at a section break. We will discuss both approaches: using galleries and manually establishing page numbering. The topic of creating complex page numbers (those that contain a chapter number plus page number or an appendix letter plus page number) will be addressed on page 87.

How to Add Page Numbering Using a Gallery

Word contains a gallery with scores of page number styles ranging from simple page numbers to complex headers or footers that contain graphic elements, text, and page numbers. You can add a page number using this gallery while either working in the document or from the header and footer editor. In the former case, once you have selected a page number style the header and footer editor automatically opens.

Step 1.   If you are in a document view, select the **Insert** tab and in the **Header & Footer** group, select the desired gallery. If you are working in the header and footer editor, the controls are located in the **Header & Footer** group associated with the **Design** tab. The following table lists the options available from the three controls.

Control	Description
Header	Contains a gallery of highly formatted headers, some of which include page numbering. You may also enter the header and footer editor by choosing **Edit Header** (if working in document view).
Footer	Similar to the Header gallery, except footers are inserted, some of which contain page numbering. Choosing **Edit Footer** enters the header and footer editor (if working in document view).
Page Number	Presents four galleries for placing a variety of page number styles. **Top of Page** and **Bottom of Page** present header and footer galleries, respectively. **Page Margins** contains a gallery of page numbering that is positioned within the either the left or right margin. **Current Position** places a relatively simple page number scheme wherever the insertion point is located in the document.

Step 2. Insert the desired page number using one of the controls outlined above. If desired, continue to manually edit the inserted page number.

Step 3. Close the header and footer editor to return to document view.

How to Manually Add a Page Number

Manually adding page numbering gives you full control over the position and format. In this example we will step through the procedure to add a *Page X of Y* style footer.

Step 1. Open the Header and Footer editor and move to the page footer.

Step 2. If desired, adjust paragraph alignment or use tab stops to create a left-aligned, centered, or right-aligned page number.

Step 3. Type the word *Page* followed by a space.

Step 4. Move to the **Insert** tab and in the **Text** group, select **Quick Parts**, then choose **Field.** The **Field** dialog box will appear:

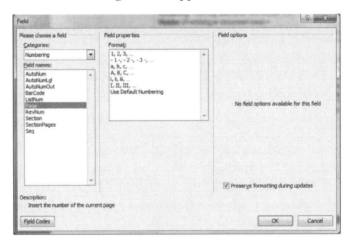

Step 5. From the **Categories** drop down box, select **Numbering**. In the **Field Names** area, select **Page**, then move to the **Format** area and select the desired format. Choose **OK** when done.

Step 6. The insertion point should be positioned to the right of the newly inserted field. Type a space, then the word *of* followed by another space.

Step 7. Return to the **Insert** group and again select **Field** from the **Quick Parts** control.

Step 8. On the **Field** dialog box, choose **Document Information** from the **Categories** drop box, then select **NumPages** from the **Field Names** list. In the **Format** area select the desired page number format, then choose **OK**.

Step 9. Make any formatting adjustments to your page number scheme.

How to Adjust Page Number Properties

The style of page numbering (for example, Arabic or lower case Roman numerals) can be changed. In addition, you can set the starting number for each section in a document.

Step 1. Open the header and footer editor, if you are working in document view.

Step 2. Select **Page Number** from the **Header & Footer** group on the **Design** tab, then choose **Format Page Number**. The **Page Number Format** dialog box will appear:

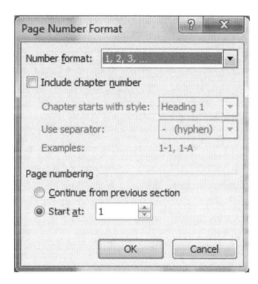

Step 3. Choose the desired **Number format**.

Step 4. If you need to include chapter numbers (for example, to number pages 2-1, 2-2, 2-3, etc.), enable **Include chapter number**. Indicate which style is used to denote each chapter, then select a separator.

Step 5. If is it necessary to restart page numbering, or to begin at some number other than 1, I, i, A, etc., select **Start at** and select a starting number.

Step 6. Choose **OK** when done.

Page number style settings are specific to sections, unless **Continue from previous section** is enabled. When enabled, this setting overrides unlinking between sections (as discussed later in this Chapter). This is necessary in order to provide continuous page numbering even though the headers and footers may otherwise appear unique between sections.

It is common practice in the publishing industry to start the first page of chapter 1 in Arabic numerals beginning with 1. Pages prior to chapter one are usually formatted in upper or lowercase Roman numerals. Thus, editors typically use the **Page Number Format** dialog box to establish these two separate numbering schemes in a printed book. This is the scheme used for all books published by Sycamore Technical Press.

General Formatting of Headers and Footers

Headers and footers appear outside of the area denoted by the page top and bottom margins. Typically, their vertical placement is relative to the physical edge of the paper while horizontally they are aligned within the section's left and right margins, although it is quite possible to move the content of a header and/or footer beyond the right and left margins. Various printers are more or less able to print to the extreme edge of the physical paper and Word may not be fully informed of a printer's limitation in this regard, so you may need to be aware that if some content of a header or footer is being cropped, physical adjustments of the header and footer (in terms of vertical placement or left/right margins) may be required on your part.

In this segment we will first discuss working with headers and footers when they are expected to appear the same throughout the document—even if the document contains many separate sections. The issue of the *Same as Previous* attribute will then be discussed, as understanding it is essential in situations which require that a header and/or footer in one portion of your document appear different from in other sections.

Warning: Novice users of Microsoft Word may think that the header and/or footer on each page within a multiple page document is a feature of that page. This is not the case. As we will discuss, each section may have at most 3 different types of headers and footers. Modifying the content of a header and/or footer within a section while on any page will change the content for the entire section. If **Same as Previous** is enabled for all sections in a multiple-section document, editing any header and/or footer will cascade through the entire document.

How to Create a Common Header or Footer for a Document

This is the default behavior in Word.

Step 1.   Select the **Insert** tab and move to the **Header & Footer** group. The following table outlines the available controls.

Option	Description
Header	Displays a gallery of predefined header types. The **Edit Header** command will open the header area for custom header creation. Once in this area you may switch between header and footer.
Footer	As above except for footers. **Edit Footer** will open the footer area for custom footer creation. Once in this editor you may switch between footer and header.
Page Number	Opens four different galleries for the creation of predefined page numbering. A gallery exists to insert a predefined page number into the header, footer, margin or current cursor location. You may also choose to **Format Page Number** to customize its appearance or **Remove Page Numbers**.

Step 2.   Select the desired option from one of the controls within the **Header & Footer** group, or to create a custom header and/or footer, choose either **Edit Header** or **Edit Footer** from their respective parent controls. A header and a footer edit area are each illustrated below:

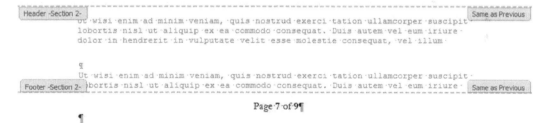

Step 3.   Manipulate the header or footer using tools available from the **Design** tab associated with **Header & Footer Tools**. Use the following table as a guide:

Group	Description
Header & Footer	These controls are the same as those found in the **Header & Footer** group on the **Insert** tab (discussed in Step 1, above).
Insert	Inserts predefined objects such as date/time fields, fields that contain document information (such as path and filename or author), pictures, or clip art.
Navigation	Move between the header and footer edit area; move between headers and footers within a section (if using different first page and/or different odd and even headers & footers); control **Same as Previous**.
Options	Set a different first page, and/or odd and even headers and footers. Also toggle the display of the body text on the document. These options are also found on the **Layout** tab of the **Page Setup** dialog box.
Position	Sets the vertical position of the header and footer, relative to the physical page edge. Also sets predefined tab stops for creating flush left, flush right, or page-centered content. Note that these settings may also be manipulated as alignment properties of the paragraph.
Close	Exits header and footer edit mode and returns you to the document.

Step 4.   Use controls from the **Header & Footer** group to insert predefined header or footer content, or create your own content as desired. For full formatting control over a header or footer, move to the **Home** and/or **Insert** tab to work with most attributes and objects which are available to a document.

Step 5.   If you need to move between the **Header** and **Footer** editing area, either scroll up or down in the document or from the **Navigation** group on the **Design** tab, select either **Go to Header** or **Go to Footer**.

Step 6.   Select **Close** from the **Design** tab associated with **Header & Footer Tools** when done.

Example: Creating a Footer with Text and Page Numbering

To illustrate how to create a custom footer, we will step through the procedure to create a footer that appears as follows:

Step 1.   Open the footer editor by choosing **Edit Footer** from the **Footer** control on the **Insert** tab. By default, the paragraph justification should be *Left* and a **Center Align** as well as a **Right Align** tab stop should be set. Note that these will disappear once you insert a predefined page number!

Step 2.   Ensure that the insertion point is to the left side of the footer edit area and type *Annual Report - January 2010*.

Step 3.   To insert a page number in the style *Page X of Y*, move to the **Page Number** control on the **Headers & Footers** group. Select **Current Position**, then choose an option from the **Page X of Y**. Word will insert a combination of text and fields in the footer.

Step 4.   With the insertion point between your typed text and the inserted page numbering, move to the ruler and create a right-aligned tab that is set at the right margin.

Step 5.   Press *Tab* to insert a tab stop. This should cause the text *Page X of Y* to be right-aligned.

Step 6.   Select the **Close** button from the **Design** tab associated with **Header & Footer Tools** when done.

How to Create a Different First Page Header or Footer

Many documents begin with a blank header or footer for the first page, or use a scheme that differentiates the first page from all other pages in the document. Word can create a **First Page Header** or **Footer** for these purposes. For the time being, the first page header or footer you create using this method will only apply to the first page of the document, regardless of whether sections are added later downstream (we will discuss this issue shortly).

If you have an existing header and/or footer and create a different first page header and footer, the first page object will be blank—even though the original header and/or footer had content. If you create a different first page header & footer in a document that lacks headers and footers, all headers and footers will be blank.

Step 1.   Open a header & footer using the previously discussed procedures.

Step 2.   In the **Options** group on the **Design** tab, select **Different First Page**. Word will insert a **First Page Header** and a **First Page Footer** in the document. A **First Page Footer** is illustrated below.

Lorem ipsum dolor sit amet, consectetuer adipiscing elit, sed diam nonummy nibh euismod tincidunt ut laoreet dolore magna aliquam erat volutpat. Ut wisi minim veniam, quis nostrud exerci tation ullamcorper suscipit

First Page Footer -Section 1-

¶

Step 3.   If desired, move between the **First Page Header** and **First Page Footer** by either scrolling through the page or by using the appropriate controls in the **Navigation** group on the **Design** tab.

Step 4.   If you wish to have content on a first page header or footer, insert predefined content using the **Header & Footer** group controls or create your own content.

Step 5.   To move to a regular **Header** or **Footer** for the rest of the document, either scroll down the page or select **Next Section** from the **Navigation** group on the **Design** tab.

Although the first page header and footer are labeled as such, the regular headers and footers for the remainder of the document will appear as those illustrated beginning on page 69.

How to Create Different Odd and Even Page Headers and Footers

This procedure is independent of creating a different first page header or footer. This independence allows you to create sophisticated header and footer designs.

Step 1.   Open a header & footer using the previously discussed procedures.

Step 2.   In the **Options** group on the **Design** tab, select **Different Odd & Even Pages**. Word will insert an **Even Page Header**, **Odd Page Header**, **Even Page Footer**, and an **Odd Page Footer** in the document. These header and footer types are illustrated below.

Removing Headers or Footers from a Document

The following table outlines the procedure to remove various types of headers and footers, as well as explains how Word reacts if the header or footer contains content:

To Remove	Procedure and Action
A standard header or footer	This procedure only applies if content is present. If so, open the desired header and/or footer and delete the content, then close the header & footer editor. If the document contains multiple sections and some sections do not have **Same as Previous** enabled, you may need to step through the sections in the document and repeat this procedure on the headers and/or footers in individual sections.
The first page header or footer	Open the header & footer editor and uncheck the **Different First Page** control in the **Options Group** (or use the **Layout** tab on the **Page Setup** dialog). The content of the first page header and/or footer will be removed. If any other header or footer types with content are present in the section, their content will migrate onto the first page (for example, the content of the **Odd Page** header and/or footer will appear if the first page is odd-numbered).
Odd/Even page header or footer	As above, except uncheck the **Different Odd & Even Pages** control. You cannot independently remove only even or odd headers and footers (except to simply delete the content in the desired type). Unchecking this control removes both types of headers *and* footers. Any content in the **Odd Page** controls will migrate into the remaining header and footer areas.

Understanding *Same as Previous* in Headers and Footers

In the previous procedures, the header or footer which were defined become the header or footer for the entire document. This behavior is regardless of whether the document has multiple sections or will have multiple sections inserted following the initial establishment of a header or footer. The reason for this is a property named **Same as Previous** (for some unexplained reason the command button in Word is instead named **Link to Previous**) which is applied by default whenever you insert a section break in a document.

This property has its good and bad points. Were it not for **Same as Previous**, for documents that may contain multiple sections yet require a common header and/or footer throughout, you'd have to work with each section separately to define the header and/or footer.

In the more detailed case where your document does require different headers and/or footers in a document, this property can become troublesome, especially if you end up inserting sections into a document where the formatting of separate headers and/or footers has already occurred.

Understanding this property and how to use it is essential when you need to create a document where headers and/or footers are different between sections. The following illustration provides a thumbnail sketch of how the **Same as Previous** property works using a three-section document.

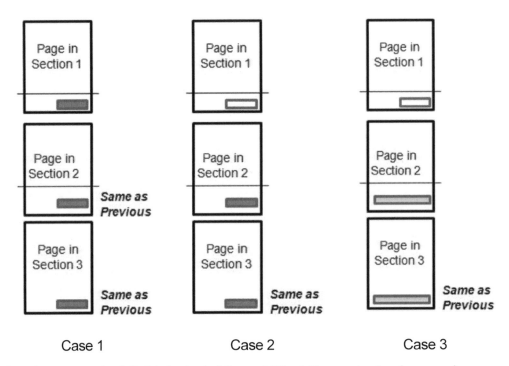

Case 1   Case 2   Case 3

Case 1 represents the default behavior in Microsoft Word. Two section breaks create three separate sections. By default, **Same as Previous** is enabled for the footers in sections 2 and 3 (section 1 *never* has **Same as Previous** since it is the topmost section). Any edit to any footer within any of the three sections will cascade to the all pages in the other sections. This behavior is useful when you need a consistent header or footer in a multipage, multi-section document.

In Case 2, the footer in section 2 has been modified so that **Same as Previous** has been disabled. This essentially unlinks section 2 from section 1. Any change to the footer in section 1 is isolated to those pages within that section only. Note that in order to create a unique footer in section 1, the **Same as Previous** attribute in section 2 required modification!

Case 3 continues the lesson from Case 2 and illustrates that section 2 and 3 are still linked since the **Same as Previous** attribute is still enabled in the footer for section 3. Thus, any change made to a footer on any page in either section 2 or 3 will cascade to the other section, but not to section 1.

Same as Previous works separately for headers and footers, so for example, it is possible to keep **Same as Previous** on for all footers to establish a common page number style, yet break **Same as Previous** for the headers in all sections so the document can contain headers that differ between sections.

How to Control Same as Previous

Recall from the discussion that to fully isolate a header or footer from one section in a large document, you must break **Same as Previous** both in the desired section *and* in the next section downward.

Step 1.   Open the **Header and Footer** editor and move to the desired section.

Step 2.   Move to the **Header** or **Footer** edit area. If you wish to break **Same as Previous** for both headers and footers, you will repeat the next step, once while in the header and again while in the footer.

Step 3.   In the **Navigation** group, toggle the **Link to Previous** control. If **Same as Previous** is active this action removes it. If not active, this action will enable it, thus linking the header and/or footer in this section to the previous one.

Complex Headers and Footers

With an introduction of the types of headers and footers Word offers, plus an understanding of the **Same as Previous** header and footer attribute, we will now delve into those cases where headers and/or footers must be different between sections of a document. First, to recap a few important points:

- The **Same as Previous** attribute must be disabled (it is enabled by default) for the footers or headers that need to be different between sections. For any given section to be fully isolated from its neighbors, its **Same as Previous** attribute *and that of its immediate downstream section* must be disabled.

- Footers and Headers behave independently, so **Same as Previous** may be enabled for footers so page numbering is consistent, and disabled for headers so chapter titles can appear within each chapter.

- The different types of headers and footers, discussed on page 63, are attributes of sections, thus various sections of your document may have different types of headers and footers. For example, the **Roman Numeral**-numbered page numbers before Chapter 1 in most books may be centered in a footer, and once you encounter Chapter 1, page numbering switches to different odd and even page format (as is the format in the print version of this book).

Creating a Section-Specific Header or Footer

There are several approaches to creating headers and/or footers that differ between sections. On one extreme, you set up headers and footers as each section is inserted in a document. The other extreme approach is to not format headers and footers until the document is close to completion (although sections have been inserted already). We will discuss each of these approaches as well as discuss how to insert a section in the middle of a document that has already been formatted for headers and footers.

One special topic which will also be discussed is working with headers and footers in landscaped sections.

How to Create Different Headers and Footers in a New Document

This procedure assumes that you will add sections serially as the document grows. The procedure focuses on establishing different headers and/or footers as soon as the section has been inserted into the document. If working with different odd/even headers and footers, only the appropriate header/footer will appear when the first page of the new section is created. You will need to add content or pages (by inserting page breaks) in order for the other header/footer to appear. This is also true if working with different first page header/footers.

Step 1.   Position the insertion point in the document at the point where a new section is needed. Insert a section break of the appropriate type (see page 54).

Step 2.   Move to the newly inserted section and open the header and footer editor (see page 69 for the procedure on opening the editor).

Step 3.   If you require a different first page header and footer (see page 71), or odd and even page headers and footers (see page 72), use either the controls on the **Options** group of the **Design** tab, or use the controls on the **Layout** tab of the **Page Setup** dialog to enable the desired header and footer type.

Step 4.   For any header or footer that must be different in the current section, first move to the desired header or footer, then from the **Options** group on the **Design** tab, deselect **Link to Previous**. The **Same as Previous** notice on the header or footer will disappear.

Step 5.   Insert the desired content into the header and/or footer.

Step 6.   As new sections may be inserted downstream within the document, repeat Steps 2 through 5.

Remember that for any header or footer that must be consistent throughout the document, keep the **Same as Previous** attribute enabled.

How to Create Different Headers and Footers in an Inserted Section

There are times when you need to insert a new section between existing sections. You will need to keep track of the section number, both of the newly inserted section and of the section immediately downstream. Recall that the **Status Bar**, first discussed on page 54, is useful for indicating the current section number.

This procedure requires you to step downward into the header & footer area of the section immediately downstream of the newly inserted one. If you do not break the downstream section's **Same as Previous** attribute, any changes you make to the inserted section will cascade downward into the next section as well.

Step 1.   Position the insertion point in the document at the point where a new section is needed. Insert a section break of the appropriate type (see page 54).

Step 2.   Move to the newly inserted section and open the header and footer editor (see page 69 for the procedure on opening the editor).

Step 3.   Note the section number of the newly inserted section. Use the **Next Section** control on the **Navigation** group of the **Design** tab (or scroll downward through the document) to step to the header & footer area for the section immediately downstream.

Step 4.   For each header and footer that must be different in the newly inserted section, break **Same as Previous** attribute by deselecting **Link to Previous**. This is necessary as any edits you make in the newly inserted section would cascade downward without first breaking this link.

Step 5.   Return to the newly inserted section and add content as desired to the header and/or footer area.

How to Create Different Headers and Footers in a Finalized Document

Some authors prefer to wait until all sections have been inserted and the document is nearing completion before headers and footers are formatted. If you choose this approach, the best way to configure different headers and/or footers between sections is to begin at the bottom of the document and work upstream. This is because **Same as Previous** works to inherit the header and/or footer content of previous (or upstream) sections. Although it is possible to work from the other direction, starting at the bottom of the document and moving toward the first section avoids potential problems by systematically isolating sections while establishing section-specific header and/or footer content.

Step 1.   Move to the end of the document and open the header and footer editor.

Step 2.   For any header or footer that must be section-specific in its content, place the insertion point within the header or footer and deselect the **Link to Previous** control on the **Navigation** group of the **Design** tab. Repeat this procedure as necessary until all section-specific headers and footers have been addressed.

Step 3.   Create the header and/or footer content for the section-specific headers and/or footers.

Step 4.   Move upward to the header and footer area of the previous section by either scrolling upward through the document or by using the **Previous Section** control on the **Navigation** group.

Step 5.   Repeat Steps 2 and 3. Continue stepping upward and repeating Steps 2 and 3 for each successive section until you reach section 1 in the document.

Step 6.   Close the header and footer editor.

Headers and Footers on Landscape Pages

When you insert a section that contains landscape pages in an otherwise portrait-oriented document, the headers and footers remain in their top-of-the-page and bottom-of-the-page orientation. This is an odd feature in Microsoft Word as the following illustration shows how such a section will appear when printed; what is generally expected in a printed document; and how to correct this issue in Word.

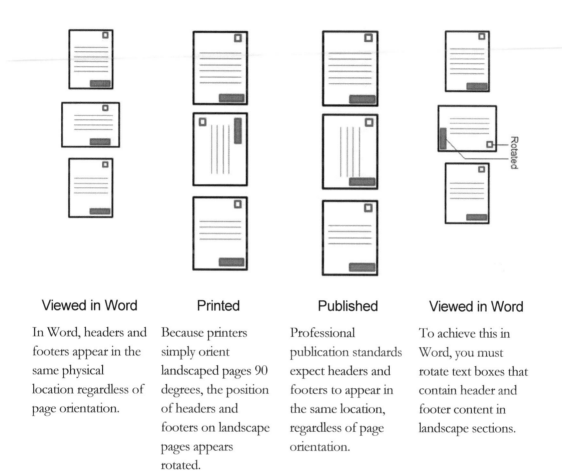

Viewed in Word	Printed	Published	Viewed in Word
In Word, headers and footers appear in the same physical location regardless of page orientation.	Because printers simply orient landscaped pages 90 degrees, the position of headers and footers on landscape pages appears rotated.	Professional publication standards expect headers and footers to appear in the same location, regardless of page orientation.	To achieve this in Word, you must rotate text boxes that contain header and footer content in landscape sections.

Rotating content in a header or footer requires use of a **Text Box** object. The standard header and footer edit area is not capable of being rotated. The key to formatting a correct header and/or footer in a landscape section is to remember that the header must be rotated downward and to the right 90° while a footer must be rotated upward and to the left by 90°.

Microsoft Word offers rotated page numbers that serve as templates for creating rotated headers and/or footers.

How to Create a Rotated Header and/or Footer for a Landscape Section

Step 1.   Move to the desired landscaped section and open the header and footer editor.

Step 2. If the **Same as Previous** attribute is enabled for any header or footer in the next downstream section, move to that section and unlink those headers and footers. Refer to the procedures in the previous section for details.

Step 3. Return to the target section and deselect **Link to Previous** to fully isolate the landscape section from the upstream section (otherwise you will end up rotating the upstream headers and/or footers as well).

Step 4. If you need to only rotate a header, skip to Step 10. To rotate a footer, first copy any content (if any exists) and delete the footer.

Step 5. Move to the **Page Number** control in the **Header & Footer** group on the **Design** tab and select **Page Margins**, then from the **Plain Number** area, select **Large Left**. A page number within a text box will appear to the left margin of the page.

Step 6. Select the text box (the border will appear when selected—be careful not to select the text within the text box instead). Right-click on the text box border and choose **Format AutoShape** from the shortcut menu.

Step 7. Move to the **Text Box** tab and ensure that **Word Wrap Text in AutoShape** is deselected and **Resize AutoShape to Fit Text** is selected. Close the dialog box.

Step 8. In the **Text** group on the **Format | Text Box Tools** tab, use the **Text Direction** control to rotate the text 90°.

Step 9. Either delete the contents of the text box and paste the footer contents you copied in Step 4 (if applicable), or type any content you require for the footer.

Step 10. If you need to rotate a header, return to the **Page Number** control in the **Header & Footer** group, and from the **Plain Number** area select **Large Right**. A page number within a text box will appear to the right margin of the page.

Step 11. Repeat Steps 6 through 9 to format the header text.

Margins on Rotated Headers and Footers

When you switch from a section with portrait oriented pages to a landscape section, Word still sees the margins for the landscape page and its headers and footers in the same orientation as if the page were still portrait. The following illustration outlines this point:

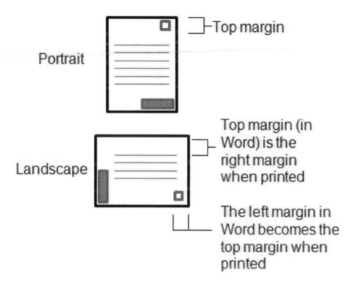

Portrait — Top margin

Landscape — Top margin (in Word) is the right margin when printed

The left margin in Word becomes the top margin when printed

If your document uses the same value for all margins, this becomes less of an issue. However, if top and bottom margins are different from the left and right margins, this essentially converts to different top and bottom margins for a landscape-oriented section since Word does not carry over margin values (e.g. swapping top margin on a portrait page to right margin on a landscape page) when you create a landscape section from a portrait one. In such cases you'll need to track these values on your own. Review the first and third images on page 79 to understand how a landscape page is treated in most publications and thus how it differs from its presentation in Microsoft Word.

How to Align Rotated Headers and Footers

This procedure requires some knowledge of the page margin settings as well as the settings that vertically align headers and footers on the portrait-oriented pages of the document. This procedure assumes that the margin settings are constant throughout your document. If not, you'll need to also adjust individual sections to ensure that headers and/or footers are consistently placed throughout.

For exact placement of rotated headers and/or footers, it is helpful to force the size of the text box containing the header or footer content to a known size. You can use this information to accurately center or right-align content.

Step 1.   If necessary, review the current margin settings for your document as well as the location of headers and footers relative to the paper's edge. To do this, move to the **Page Layout** tab and in the **Page Setup** group, click on the **Dialog Expander** to open the **Page Setup** dialog. The margin settings will appear on the **Margins** tab, while the positioning for headers and footers is on the **Layout** tab.

Step 2.   To accurately center or right-align rotated content force the **Height** of the text box to a specific size large enough to contain its content. Select the text box, then right-click and choose **Format AutoShape** from the shortcut menu. On the **Format AutoShape**, move to the **Size** tab. The dialog box will appear similar to the following:

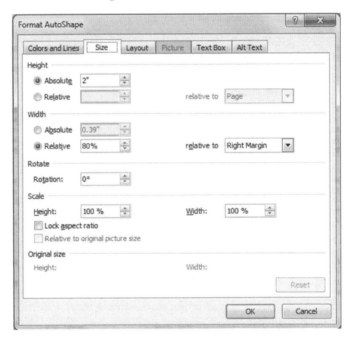

Step 3.   Adjust the **Height** (remember that the box is rotated so height equates to width once the page is rotated during printing) to **Absolute** and set a size (use units of measure appropriate for the paper size—example, inches or mm).

Step 4.   Position the text box by choosing the **Layout** tab, then select **Advanced**. The **Advanced Layout** dialog box will appear similar to the following:

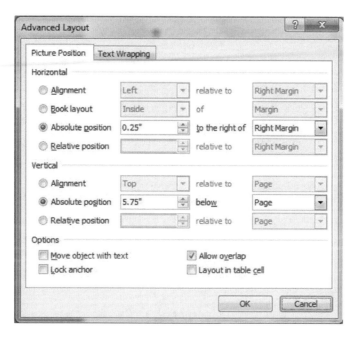

Step 5.   Modify the **Horizontal** and/or **Vertical** alignment using the following table as a guide.

Rotated Header on Landscape Page	Settings/Adjustments
Header - top right	This converts to a header at the top right corner of the page when printed. Set **Horizontal** position to **Absolute** and adjust to a value greater than zero relative to the right of the **Right Margin**. For the **Vertical** position set the value equal to the height of the landscaped page (this is the width property when the page is in portrait orientation) minus the height of the text box as set in Step 4). The paragraph orientation for the text box should be *Flush right*.
Header - top left	When printed, this header will appear flush left on the top of the page. The **Horizontal** settings are as above but the **Vertical** settings should equal the top margin setting and should be set below the **Page**.
Header - centered	The **Horizontal** positioning is as above. For the **Vertical** setting, enter a value that equals one half of the page width minus one half of the text box height as specified in Step 4. The paragraph orientation for the text box should be *Center*.

Rotated Footer on Landscape Page	Settings/Adjustments
Footer - bottom right	This converts to a footer at the bottom right corner of the page when printed. Set **Horizontal** position to **Absolute** and adjust to a value greater less than zero relative to the right of the **left Margin**. For the **Vertical** position set the value equal to the height of the landscaped page (this is the width property when the page is in portrait orientation minus the height of the text box as set in Step 4). The paragraph orientation for the text box should be *Flush right*.
Footer - bottom left	When printed, this footer will appear flush left on the bottom of the page. The **Horizontal** settings are as above but the **Vertical** settings should equal the top margin setting and should be set below the **Page**.
Footer - centered	The **Horizontal** positioning is as above. For the **Vertical** setting, enter a value that equals one half of the page width minus one half of the text box height as specified in Step 4. The paragraph orientation for the text box should be *Center*.

Step 6.   Close the dialog box by choosing **OK**. Test the final orientation by printing the document. You may wish to only print a page before and a page after the section break which switches page orientation.

 Note that there are additional attributes which may affect absolute positioning of rotated text in a text box. Although the default settings for internal padding within the text box is small, if set to a higher value the calculations outlined in the previous table will not work correctly.

How to Save Rotated Headers and Footers

It remains a mystery as to why authors have had to follow the previous procedures when working with landscape pages in Microsoft Word for multiple versions of the software. One improvement is the ability to save objects as **Building Blocks**, and you may find it convenient to do this once you have created a rotated header and/or footer that meets your needs.

Step 1.   Open the header and footer editor and select the text box or boxes in the rotated header and/or footer (hold down the *Shift* key to select multiple items).

Step 2.   From the **Headers & Footers Tools | Design** tab, in the **Header & Footer** group, choose **Header** or **Footer** (if working with both the choice doesn't matter), then select **Save Selection to (Header or Footer) Gallery**. The **Create Building Block** dialog box will appear:

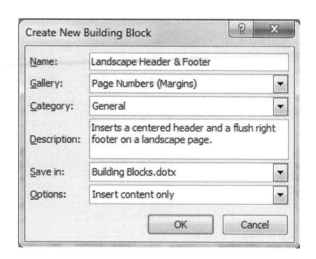

Option	Description
Name	A descriptive name for your new building block.
Gallery	For this procedure, choose *Page Numbers (Margins)* although note that this control lists all of the gallery types available in Microsoft Word.
Category	For the selected gallery, this control lists the available categories. For example, besides *General*, the *Page Numbers* category also lists *Plain Number, Page X, Plain Number*, etc. Categories cluster building blocks within their galleries.
Description	Use to provide a description of your building block.
Save in	Select the template to store the building block in. The default is the building blocks template.
Options	There are three options, although for this purpose choose *Insert content only*. The other options *Insert content in its own page* isolates the building block with page breaks while *Insert in own paragraph* isolates the building block as a separate paragraph.

Step 3.   Choose **OK** when done.

How to Use a Custom Rotated Header and Footer Building Block

Once you've saved a custom landscape header and/or footer building block, adding one to other sections of a document or into a new document is easy.

Step 1.   Open the Header and Footer editor for the desired landscape section.

Step 2.   Unlink the header and/or footer from the previous section as needed.

Step 3.　Move to the **Header & Footer** group on the **Design** tab (**Header & Footer tools)** and choose **Page Number**, then select **Page Numbers (Margins)** (note, this maps to your choice of **Gallery** in the previous procedure).

Step 4.　Select your custom building block from the appropriate gallery (also related to your choice for **Gallery** in the previous procedure). The custom header and/or footer will appear in your document.

 Building Blocks are discussed more fully in Chapter 5.

Relinking Headers or Footers

On occasion you may find it necessary to relink a header or footer to those of the previous section. When you do this, the content of the current header or footer is replaced with the content on the previous section header or footer.

Step 1.　Position the insertion point in the section you wish to relink and open the header and footer editor.

Step 2.　If relinking a header, move to the header area (if relinking a footer, move to that area and if relinking both header and footer, repeat this procedure once for each section).

Step 3.　On the **Design** tab (**Header & Footer Tools)**, in the **Navigation** group, select **Link to Previous**. The following warning will appear:

Step 4.　Choose **Yes** to relink or **No** to abandon the operation.

Troubleshooting Headers and Footers

Most problems involving headers and footers derive from working with sections. If you are working with a multi-section document and the header and/or footer content you define for each section isn't sticking, it's a section issue. On the more trivial side, header or footer content that appears eclipsed or cut off is an issue of positioning. The most common types of issues are summarized below.

- **My headers and/or footers keep changing on me!** This is clearly a situation where one or more header or footer sections have **Same as Previous** enabled. Move to the bottom of the document and enter the header and footer editor. Step upwards through the document (using the **Previous Section** command) and make sure that **Same as Previous** is not enabled for any section that must be different from its neighboring sections. Remember that both the target section and the section immediately downstream must have this property disabled.

- **Part of my header or footer content is clipped**. Ensure that the margins in either the header or footer area don't exceed the printer's physical limit for printing to the edge of a sheet. If the header or footer content is in a text box, ensure that it is located within the page margins.

- **Page numbering isn't correct. Chapter 1 begins on page 14!** The settings for the **Page Number Format** are not correct for the section that contains chapter 1. In that section, make sure that the **Start at** control is enabled and that the desired starting page number is selected. You may need to step through each section in your document to ensure that this setting only applies on your "first" page and that all downstream sections have page numbering set to **Continue from previous section**.

Complex Page Numbering

This type of page number is used by some organizations either to format page numbers in the form *Chapter number - page number* or to denote pages in an appendix as being special, for example *Appendix letter - page number*. In either case you associate a multi-level list with a particular heading style. Configured this way, the heading style automatically increments each time it is applied. For example, if the *Heading 1* style is linked to a multi-level list that is set to display the term *Chapter* followed by a number, begin at 1, and increment by 1, then each instance of the *Heading 1* style will include an auto number that increments in the manner *Chapter 1, Chapter 2, Chapter 3*, etc. When used in this way, page numbers can hook onto the auto number associated with the *Heading 1* style to present a scheme such as 1-1, 1-2, 1-3 for the first three pages of Chapter 1, or 2-1, or 2-15 for the first page of Chapter 2 (in the second example—2-15— page numbering simply continues from the previous section).

We will step through two examples. In the first, we will associate a built-in multilevel list style with the *Heading 1* style so we can auto number chapters as well as apply a chapter-page numbering scheme in a footer. In the second example, we will establish a custom multilevel list style so we can use the *Heading 8* style to denote appendices, both for auto-incrementing the appendix title and to apply a page numbering scheme such as A-1, A-2, A-3, B-1, etc.

Creating Complex Page Numbering Using a Built-in Multilevel List Style

In this example we will associate an existing multilevel list style with the *Heading 1* style. When applied to chapter titles we will be able to use a scheme for page numbering that associates chapter number with page number.

Step 1.   Position the insertion point where you intend to label the beginning of a chapter.

Step 2.   From the **Home** tab, in the **Paragraph** group, choose the **Multilevel List** control. In the **List Library** select the list style that begins with **Chapter**. Word will insert the term **Chapter 1** into your document (provided there are no other entries in the *Heading 1* style upstream in your document). If desired, type a space and any additional text you wish to use for the chapter heading.

Step 3.   To label additional chapters, insert a **Next Page Section Break** or move to a point immediately downstream of an existing break and apply the *Heading 1* style. Word will insert the text **Chapter X**, where X reflects the number of instances that the *Heading 1* style has been applied upstream of the current point. Again, type additional text to label your chapter as needed.

Step 4.   To employ chapter number - page number numbering style move to the header and footer editor and insert page numbering.

Step 5.   From the **Design** tab move to the **Header & Footer** group and select **Page Number**, then select **Format Page Number**. The **Format Page Number** dialog box will appear. It is illustrated on page 67.

Step 6.   Enable **Include Chapter Number**, and ensure that *Heading 1* is the style selected in the **Chapter starts with style** drop down box. Choose a separator if desired.

Step 7.   Choose **OK**. The page number will update to reflect the new numbering scheme.

For Chapter 1, you may wish to start page numbering with *1*. For each subsequent chapter you should choose whether to begin with *1* (the most common approach) or whether to make page numbering continuous from Chapter 1. Restarting page numbering was discussed on page 67.

When you create a table of contents (discussed in Chapter 8), the page numbering in the table will reflect the chapter number - page number style applied in the document.

Creating Complex Page Numbering Using a Custom List Style

Custom here means we will not choose an existing multilevel list style. The custom multilevel list must still be associated with an existing style, typically a header style. In this example, we will create a multilevel list that increments by letter (A, B, C, etc.) and appends the number with the term *Appendix*. We will associate it with *Heading 8* and apply it to appendices in a document.

Step 1.   Position the insertion point immediately downstream of a **Next Page Section Break** used to isolate the body of the document from the first page of what will become Appendix A.

Step 2.   On the **Home** tab, in the **Paragraph** group, select **Multilevel List**, then choose **Define new multilevel list**. The **Define New Multilevel List** dialog box will appear similar to the following:

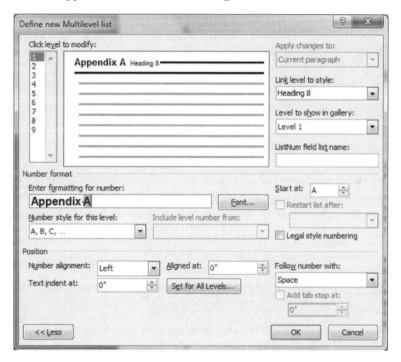

Step 3.   In the **Enter formatting for number** text box, type *Appendix* followed by a space.

Step 4.   In the **Number style for this level** drop down box, choose the *A, B, C, …* numbering style.

Step 5.   Use the **Font** command to format the number style. For example, if you wish that your appendix titles have the same format as chapter titles, adjust the font characteristics here to mirror those applied to the *Heading 1* style.

Step 6.   Lastly, choose *Heading 8* in the **Link level to style** drop down box. Choose **OK** when done. Word will insert the text *Appendix A* at the insertion point. Type any additional text required to create a heading for the appendix.

Step 7.   For any additional appendices, first insert a **Next page section break** to isolate the appendices, then begin your appendix by applying the *Heading 8* style. Word will automatically insert the text *Appendix X* where X is the letter corresponding to the number of times in your document that the *Heading 8* style has previously been applied.

Step 8.   To create the page numbering in the style *appendix letter - page number*, insert a page number into one of your appendices. Open the Header and Footer editor and from the **Header & Footer** group, choose **Page Number**, then **Format Page Number.**

Step 9.   Enable **Include Chapter Number**, and ensure that *Heading 8* is the style selected in the **Chapter starts with style** drop down box. Choose a separator if desired.

Step 10.   Choose **OK**. The page number will update to reflect the new numbering scheme.

 It is generally accepted that if you employ a page numbering scheme that notes appendix letter followed by page number, you should begin each appendix with page number *1*. Restarting page numbering was discussed on page 67.

 When you create a table of contents (discussed in Chapter 8) and associate the *Heading 8* style with a TOC level, the page numbering in the table will reflect the appendix letter - page number style applied in the document.

Columns

Whenever you require your text stream to run as two or more columns across a page you generally use columns, which are an attribute of a section. There are other approaches to accomplishing a column-like formation such as using a table or placing text in one or more text boxes. The latter approach is used in desktop publishing and is beyond the scope of this book. Using tables to achieve a column-like layout is not recommended as you lose the ability for your text to automatically flow though the column structure.

When you work with columns, you generally begin and end the column-formatted portion of a document by using the **Continuous** section break. This break permits you to switch between formats—such as mixing 1 and 2 column formatting on a single page. When you insert an automatically-generated index that uses 2 or more columns, Word automatically inserts **Continuous** section breaks (Indices are discussed in Chapter 8).

Since columns can in theory interrupt normal text flow within a document, or begin with an existing section break, the following points highlight how columns behave when inserted into an existing document.

- If you insert columns (using the **Columns** control, **page Setup** group, **Page Layout** tab), the inserted columns only apply to the current section but all text content within that section will adopt column formatting. You may override this feature by working directly with the **Columns** dialog box.

- Inserting columns into the last section of a document and then adding an additional section will cause the column formatting to be inherited by the new section.

- In an existing document, in order to insert column formatting between existing, non-column text, insert two section breaks and only apply column formatting to the section between the new breaks. Remember that a **Continuous** section break is useful if you wish to mix column and non-column formatting on a single page.

As with many objects in Microsoft Word, columns may be inserted using a predefined gallery of column styles. However, you achieve your greatest control (and understanding) of columns by working with them manually.

We will first review how to insert columns using a gallery. Discussion will then continue with working with columns using manual means.

How to Insert a Column Using a Gallery

As noted above, if you apply this procedure within an existing section, the column formatting only applies to that section. If applied at the last section in a document and then an additional section is inserted downstream, column formatting is inherited by the new section.

Step 1.   Position the insertion point at the point in the document where you wish to establish column formatting.

Step 2.   On the **Page Layout** tab, in the **Page Setup** group, choose **Columns**.

Step 3.   Select one of the five predefined columns.

How to Insert a Column Manually

This procedure gives you far greater control over column formatting. If you need to modify an existing column, position the insertion point within the column structure and proceed with Step 2.

Step 1.   Follow the first two steps from the previous procedure.

Step 2.   From the **Columns** control, choose **More Columns**. The **Columns** dialog box will appear:

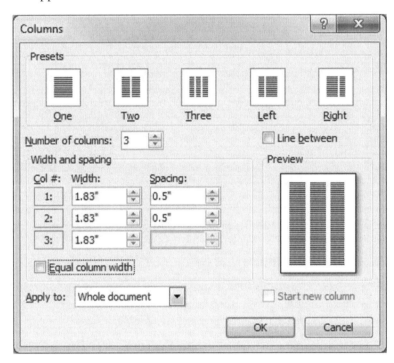

Step 3.   Select the number of columns and make adjustments using the following table as a guide.

Option	Description
Number of columns	Specify the number of columns. Choosing *1* turns off column formatting. Use this setting if you need to remove column formatting from a section.
Width and spacing	Sets the width of individual columns. If **Equal column width** is checked, you set a single column width plus a single spacing value (the space to the right of each but the last column). If **Equal column width** is unchecked, you may manually set column and spacing widths for each column.
Equal column width	Controls whether columns and spacing are equal or not.
Apply to	Sets the scope of the column formatting. The default is *This section* although the other options are *Entire Document* and *This point forward*. The latter option forces a **Continuous** section break.
Start new column	If **Apply to** is set to *This point forward*, checking this control forces the column formatting to begin at the next page.

Step 4.   Make adjustments as desired. As you change column settings the effect will appear in the **Preview** area. Choose **OK** when done.

How to Delete a Column Format

You can reduce the number of columns in order to delete one or more. By reducing the column count to *1*, you effectively remove column formatting. Removing one or more columns only rearranges text flow. No text is lost in the process.

Step 1.   With the insertion point in the target column formatting area, use any of the previous procedures to open the **Column** dialog box.

Step 2.   Reduce the number of columns (to remove one column from a multi-column format), or set the column number to *1* to remove all columns from the text stream.

Step 3.   If necessary, adjust the scope of the change by modifying the **Apply to** drop down box.

Step 4.   Choose **OK** when done.

Examples of Sections

We've reviewed the attributes of sections as they relate to the structure of a complex document. It is perfectly possible to create a document which consists of hundreds of pages yet maintains a single section. More likely are those scenarios alluded to in this Chapter that demand different page orientation, header or footer schemes, different page numbering styles, or features in a document that tend to map to either chapters in a document or to the specialty items such as glossaries or appendices.

A publication-quality book typically contains elements such as text before a table of contents (copyright page, preface, etc.), the table of contents, an introduction, individual chapters, and perhaps terminating structures such as a glossary, an index, and one or more appendices. Generally each of these units of text requires a separate section. This is especially true if the content of a header or footer also changes with glossaries, indices, or appendices.

In this segment we will summarize the discussion of sections by including a few real-world examples and how they are implemented.

Copyright Page, Preface, and Table of Contents

These are just a few of the element types which may appear before the main body of text in a document. Other items may include acknowledgements and editor's or author's notes. Although many different stylistic conventions exist, in general the pages of a document which appear before the first page of the first chapter are either not page numbered, or use a separate numbering scheme (such as Roman numerals in an otherwise Arabic-numbered document). The following section gives a few examples and outlines how to implement the requirement using sections.

Pages before Chapter One - no Headers or Footers

In this scenario you need a section break to separate the pages before Chapter One from Chapter One and all subsequent chapters. In Chapter One, headers and footers are unlinked from the previous section, and the first section lacks any headers or footers. Section one contains the un-numbered pages (such as copyright, introduction, and table of contents) and page numbering begins with Chapter One, which is in section two. If you require that Chapter One begins on page one, use the **Page Number Format** dialog to begin that section's page numbering with *1*. Some editors desire that Chapter One page numbering reflects the physical page count up to that point. In this case, leave **Continue from previous section** enabled. Despite the fact that no page numbers are formatted in the previous section, page numbering in Chapter One will reflect the actual page count up to that point.

Pages before Chapter One - Unique Headers and/or Footers

Structurally similar to the previous case except there is header and/or footer content in section one. The **Same as Previous** link is still broken between Sections one and two. You may need to adjust the page number format using the **Page Number Format** dialog box, for both sections, and to reestablish page numbering in Section two (Chapter One). This is a typical scenario where the pages prior to Chapter One are numbered using Roman numerals. Chapter One begins with Arabic numeral *1*.

In the event that you require a consistent header or footer that runs between these two sections, ensure that the **Same as Previous** attribute is enabled for the desired header or footer in section two.

Book Chapters

Anytime you create a document that requires chapters which in one way or another are different from one another, you'll use sections.

Chapters with a Consistent Page Numbering Scheme

In this simple example you accept the default value of **Same as Previous** when you add sections to your document. When you establish a page numbering scheme—either in a header or a footer—the scheme cascades automatically through the document's sections. The alternative to this approach is to use page breaks between chapters which keeps all chapters within the same section. Only use this scheme if you are certain that chapter differences in either headers or footers isn't required.

Chapters with Consistent Page Numbering and Unique Chapter Identifiers

Many books use this scheme where page numbering is consistent, but either the header or footer also contains unique text that, for example, repeats the chapter title. This is implemented by ensuring that the header or footer containing page numbering has **Same as Previous** enabled for all sections requiring consistent page numbering and the header or footer area used for chapter-specific text has this attribute disabled.

Chapters with Unique Page Numbering

The printed version of this book uses this scheme. You may wish to combine page numbering with the chapter title in a header or footer (if you only require that the chapter number change, refer to page 67 as section numbering overrides **Same as Previous**).

To enforce this scheme, ensure that the desired header and/or footer in every section has **Same as Previous** disabled. As previously discussed in the troubleshooting section, you may find it easier to format this scheme after the majority of the document has been created and work from the last section upward in the document, formatting the chapter-unique header and/or footer content section by section.

Indices, Glossaries and Appendices

These are the terminating sections in a complex document and may, like chapters, require unique headers and/or footers. Treat these sections like chapters and only enforce **Same as Previous** where consistency in a header or footer is required. Generally these sections continue page numbering, although some editors require that appendices begin with a special numbering format (such as A-1, A-2, B-1,…etc.). In this case, remember to reset page numbering at the beginning of each section that defines an appendix to the main document.

Chapter 5 | Templates

A template is a file that serves to define the general structure and style gallery for subsequent documents. All Microsoft Word documents are based on a template. If you create a simple document by default it is based on a template named **normal.dotx**. Word also ships with a large gallery of built-in templates, and you can search Microsoft's website for many more. In addition, you can easily create your own templates.

Templates do several things:

- They can contain preformatted text, headers, footers, water marks, paper size and source, and nearly any element that you can place in a regular document. This makes templates very useful for documents that require preformatted text, such as fax cover letters, letterhead stationery, and reports. Nearly any type of document you regularly create is a candidate for a template.

- Templates can store styles, macros, building blocks, and keyboard shortcuts—providing the end user with a highly customizable authoring environment.

There are over 30 installed templates and countless more available on-line from Microsoft. There is no limit to the number of templates you can create. Many authors create templates for use with the general documents that define their work. Templates are also extensively used by many large organizations to standardize the appearance of their documents.

Using Templates

As mentioned, if you simply create a blank document in Microsoft Word, it is based on the **normal.dotx** template. When you create a new document, Word offers many categories of templates, including the stock installed templates, your customized templates, and a myriad of categories of templates available from the Microsoft website.

When a document is based on a template Word essentially copies the attributes of the template into a new blank document. The blank document by default has the **docx** file extension and will be saved to a location different from that storing the template.

How to Create a New Document Based on a Template (2007)

Step 1.   Select the **Office Button** from within Microsoft Word.

Step 2.   Choose **New**. The **New Document** dialog box will appear similar to the following image:

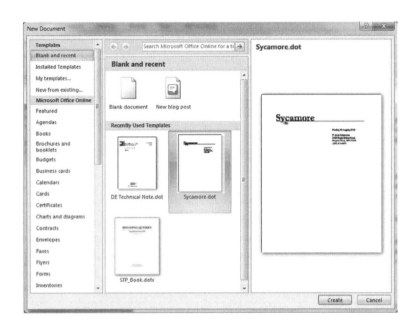

Area	Description
Templates	Organizes the templates installed locally. The **Installed Templates** link will display the installed stock templates, while **My templates** opens a gallery of any template you have created (if you create folders to house templates by category, Word will organize your templates based on folder name). The **New from existing** command does not open a template—it copies an existing document and opens the copy.
Microsoft Office Online	Features a broad list of categories, each of which will display available templates.
Blank and recent	The **Blank document** creates a new blank document based on **normal.dotx**. Any recently used templates also appear in this area.
Recently Used Templates	Summarizes any recently-used templates.

Step 3.   Select the desired template, then choose **Create**.

How to Create a New Document Based on a Template (2010/2013)

For some reason Microsoft has chosen to not incorporate any custom templates you created in earlier versions into the list of available templates. Using Word 2010 or 1013 you must first force Word to use the folder where any previously-created custom templates have been stored in order to include them in this procedure. If you choose not to follow this initial step, the only templates you may choose from when you create a new document are those offered by Microsoft, which includes the **normal** template.

How to Create a New Document Based on a Microsoft Template (2010/2013)

Step 1.   Select the **File** tab, then choose **New.** The list of available templates will appear similar to the following:

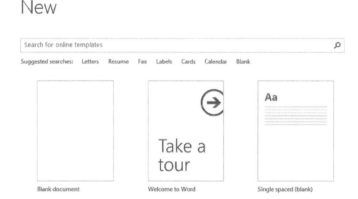

Step 2.   Select the desired template from the list (**Blank document**) is the **normal** template, or enter a search term in the search box, or select a template category from the list underneath the search box.

How to Configure Word to Display your Custom Templates (2010/2013)

The first step requires that you work with Microsoft Windows. You need to determine where templates are stored in order to configure Word. This procedure may only work on standalone computers. If you are part of a network computing environment you may need the assistance of your system administrator.

Step 1.   Select the Windows **Start button**. In the search box, type *Run.* The **Run** command box will appear.

Step 2.   In the **Open** text box, type *%appdata%\Microsoft\Templates*, then choose OK. A file explorer will open and display the contents of your template folder.

Step 3.   If the full path to the current folder isn't displayed in the **Location** bar of the file explorer, right click in the location bar and select **Edit address**. Once the full path to the template folder is displayed, select it and press *Ctrl C* to copy it. Close the file dialog box and return to Microsoft Word.

Step 4.   In Word, choose **File**, then **Options**. Move to the **Save** area.

Step 5.   Position the insertion point in the **Default personal templates location** text box and type *Ctrl V* to paste the contents copied in Step 3.

Step 6.   Choose **OK** to close the dialog box, then restart Word.

How to Create a New Document Based on a Custom Template (2010/2013)

You must follow the previous procedure to inform Word where your custom templates are located before you can use this procedure.

Step 1.   Select the **File** tab, then choose **New**.

Step 2.   Below the search text area, select **Personal**. Any templates stored in the file location specified in the previous procedure will be listed. If there are subfolders, these will be listed as well.

Step 3.   Navigate to the desired template and select it.

Creating and Modifying Templates

The power in using templates is the ability to create your own in order to best tailor document types to fit your needs. Creating a template is essentially identical to creating a document except when you save your document. Modifying a template requires opening the template itself (not opening a document based on the template).

How to Create a Template

Step 1.   Begin with a new, blank document (which will be based on the **normal.dotx** template), or create a new document based on another existing template. The latter option will transfer any styles and/or macros that may be associated with the existing template.

Step 2.   Create any content as you desire. Templates may contain header and footer content, text in the body of the document, inserted tables, form fields, and any element that you can insert in a document.

Step 3.   Make any desired adjustments to the physical properties of the document, such as paper size, page orientation, margins, paper source (printer option), etc.

Step 4.   Create any styles you wish to associate with the template. When you define each new style, ensure that the **New documents based on this template** radio button is selected.

Step 5.   Assign any custom keyboard shortcuts if desired. Again when using the **Customize Keyboard** dialog, ensure that the new keyboard assignments are stored to the current document.

Step 6. To create the template, select the **Save** button (only if the document is unnamed), or from the **Office** button, select **Save As...**

Step 7. If using Word 2007, in the **Organize** area, select **Templates**. If using Word 2010 or 2013, when you select the document type in the next step Word will automatically move to the correct folder.

Step 8. In the **Save as type** drop down box, select either **Word Template (.dotx)** or, if the template contains macros, choose **Word Macro-Enabled Template (dotm)**.

Step 9. If desired, choose **New Folder** and create a folder to contain the template.

Step 10. Provide a descriptive name for your template, then choose **Save**.

Step 11. Save the template.

 If you choose to create a new folder in Step 9, Word will organize your templates into categories defined by the folder name.

How to Modify an Existing Template

This procedure opens the template so you can make changes directly to the document. Note that many actions in Microsoft Word such as creating or modifying an existing style or recording a macro offer the ability to save the changes to the underlying template—thus there are other ways to modify a template without opening it.

Step 1. Select the **Office Button** (2007) or select **File** (2010/2013). For users of Word 2007, follow Steps 2 through 4, then skip to Step 7. For users of Word 2010 or 2013, begin with Step 5.

Step 2. Choose **Open**. The **Open Document** dialog box will appear.

Step 3. Select **Templates**, then navigate to the desired template.

Step 4. Select the template and choose **Open**. Word will open the template. Jump to Step 7 to continue.

Step 5. Choose **Open**. Select either your computer or the appropriate storage location (this should be the location specified in the procedure beginning on page 99). Choose **Browse**, then navigate to the folder containing your templates.

Step 6. Select the desired template and choose **Open**. Word will open the template.

Step 7. Make the desired changes to the document.

Step 8.   **Save** the document or choose **Save as..** to retain the original template design and save the changes to a new template.

Templates as Containers

Beyond their role as a skeletal structure for a wide variety of document types, templates can serve as containers for other elements such as styles, macros, keyboard shortcuts, and building blocks. In the majority of cases you must pay attention when defining such an element to ensure that you locate it in the desired template. Word offers an organizer that allows you to migrate styles and macros between various templates.

The power of using various templates to contain customizable elements is that you can reduce the clutter in **normal.dotx** and isolate styles, macros, keyboard short cuts, and building blocks. The objects which are unique to a specific need, such as working with a fax cover letter or creating an annual report, are isolated to templates designed to support those document types. Thus, you or your organization may require 20 work-related styles, yet they can be contained such that they are grouped within templates that reflect their document-related need.

Styles

When you define a new style or modify an existing one you have the option of saving changes either to the current document or to all documents based on the current template (see page 36 to review this procedure). To create a style that is associated with a template you have three choices:

- Create or modify a style in a document based on the target template and choose to save the style so all documents based on the current template are affected. This approach was discussed on page 38.

- Create or modify a style while the target template is open and is the current document.

- Use the **Organizer** to migrate styles between documents. The **Organizer** was introduced on page 39.

Custom Keyboard Shortcuts and Macros

Any macro you record may be stored in the current document, in **normal.dotx** (which makes the macro available to all documents based on that template), or another template if the current document isn't based on **normal.dotx**. Macros may be moved between documents and templates using the **Organizer** which was introduced on page 39.

How to Store Custom Keyboard Shortcuts in a Template

To store a keyboard shortcut in a template other than **normal.dotx**, open the target template or create a new document based on the target template.

Step 1. In Word 2007 select the **Office Button**, (in Word 2010/13 choose **File**) then choose **Word Options**.

Step 2. On the **Word Options** dialog box, select **Customize**, then in the **Keyboard Shortcuts** area, choose **Customize...** The **Keyboard Shortcuts** dialog box will appear similar to the following:

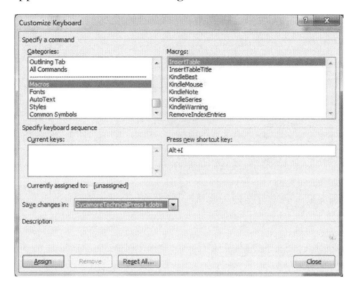

Step 3. Select the category of action and then the specific action. In the illustration above, a macro named *InsertTable* is assigned the ***Alt I*** keystroke combination.

Step 4. Select the desired template from the **Save changes in** drop down box.

Step 5. Select **Assign**, then choose **Close**.

How to Store Macros in a Template

The creation of macros is beyond the scope of this book, however you may need to attach macros to a template so this procedure is included. Macros are stored in a Visual Basic for Applications *module*. When a document contains a macro it must be saved as a **macro-enabled document** and will have the **docm** file extension (rather than the macro-less **docx** file extension). Templates that contain macros likewise must be saved as a **macro-enabled template** and will use the **dotm** file extension rather than the standard **dotx** file extension.

There are two ways to associate a macro with a template. While creating the macro you may assign it to the target template or you can use the **Organizer** to move macros between templates and/or documents.

How to Store a New Macro in a Template

Either open the target template, or use a document based on it before proceeding.

Step 1.   From the **View** tab, in the **Macros** group, select **Record Macro**. The **Record Macro** dialog box will appear:

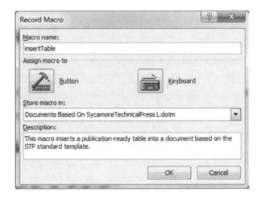

Step 2.   Define the characteristics of the macro. Before you begin recording, select the target template from the **Store macro in** drop down box.

Step 3.   Choosing **OK** will start macro recording while **Cancel** will abandon its creation. If you proceed to record remember to stop recording by choosing **Stop Recording** from the **Macro** command.

How to Organize Existing Macros

The **Organizer** was introduced on page 39. This tool only migrates or copies *modules*, which are objects that contain one or more macros. By default macros are stored in a module named *Module 1* (unless you use the VBA editor to create new modules or rename the default one).

Step 1.   If not visible, open the **Styles** pane (use the **Dialog Expander** on the **Styles** group or press *Alt Ctrl Shift S*).

Step 2.   At the bottom of the **Styles** pane, select **Manage Styles**.

Step 3.   Choose **Import/Export**. On the **Organizer** select the **Macro Project Items** tab. The dialog box will appear similar to the following:

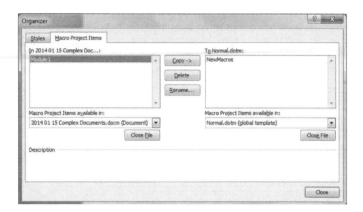

The controls on the left-hand side of the **Macro** tab generally relate to the current document, while the right-hand controls relate to the underlying template. The source and destination files can be changed by use of the **Close File** button.

Option	Description
In / To *filename*	Names the current document. This can change by using the **Close File** command. The prefix *In* and *To* may also toggle depending upon which macro window is used to select a module to move.
Styles available in	Lists the modules available in the document named above the list window. Also lists the document serving as the source for the style list.
Close File	Closes the document and toggles to an **Open File** command. Use this to choose another document or template to act as a source or target to move styles.
Copy	Copies the selected file to the other document. The direction of the copy operation depends upon whether a module was selected from the left or right side of the dialog box.
Delete	Deletes the selected module.
Rename	Renames the selected module. This is useful if you are importing a module into a document that contains a module of the same name.

Step 4.   Use the previous table as a guide to direct how modules are exported or imported. If the source or target document isn't available, choose **Close File**, then **Open File** and select another document or template.

Step 5.   Select **Close** when done.

Building Blocks

This document element was introduced into Microsoft Word a few versions ago. A building block is any predefined or custom item that has an associated gallery. Major building blocks include headers, footers, page numbers, tables, text boxes, and watermarks. Beginning with Word 2007, building blocks are no longer stored in **normal.dotx** but in a specialized template named **Building Blocks.dotx**. However, like styles and macros, you can create custom building blocks and store them in any template of your choice.

Building blocks are useful when you frequently work with a snippet of text, tables with a defined structure, or other components of a document that may appear many times. By defining a building block once it becomes a quickly insertable element that is available to all of your documents.

There are two ways to associate a building block with a particular template. When you first create a building block you can choose the storage location. Existing building blocks may be moved using the **Building Blocks Organizer**. In either case, the target template, or a document based on the target template must be open before proceeding.

How to Store a New Building Block in a Template

This procedure will create a new table building block but the process of locating a new building block in a desired template is the same regardless of building block type.

Step 1.   Create the desired content which will become a building block, or select existing content.

Step 2.   On the **Insert** tab, in the **Text** group, choose **Quick Parts**, then select **Save Selection to Quick Part Gallery**. The **Create New Building Block** dialog box will appear similar to the following:

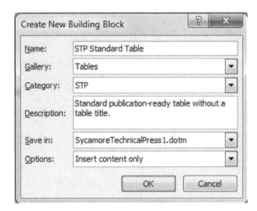

Step 3.   Provide a name for the Building Block, choose an appropriate **Gallery**, and select an existing **Category** or create a new one (this will control where in the selected gallery the Building Block will appear), and lastly provide some descriptive text.

Step 4.   To locate the Building Block in the desired template, select it from the list of templates using the **Save in** drop down box.

Step 5.   Choose the appropriate insert **Option**. Use the table on page 85 as a guide.

Step 6.   Select **OK** when done. The Building Block will be available to any document based on the target template.

How to Organize Existing Building Blocks

Use this procedure to move existing Building Blocks. If you wish to move a building block to a custom template, that template or a document created from it must be open.

Step 1.   From the **Insert** menu, in the **Text** group select **Quick Parts**, then choose **Building Blocks Organizer...** The **Building Blocks Organizer** will appear similar to the following:

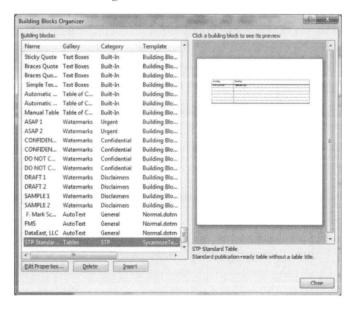

Step 2.   Select the desired Building Block from the list, then select **Edit Properties**. The **Modify Building Block** dialog box will appear (it is identical to the illustration from the previous procedure).

Step 3.   Use the **Save in** drop down box to relocate the building block to the target template.

Step 4.   Select **OK**.

Chapter 6 | Working with Tables

Tables are distinct elements in a Word document. They are cellular structures where one or more rows and one or more columns define a grid of cells, each of which may contain content such as text, graphics, objects, or even other tables. By default, all cells within a table share the same formatting properties although it is easy to configure individual cells to maintain separate properties.

Table Basics

Tables consist of one or more rows and one or more columns that define a grid structure. The intersection of a column and row maps to a cell, which is the fundamental unit of organization in a table. The regular grid nature of a table may be interrupted by merging two or more cells together. By default, a table is treated as a large text element and will flow with the text that surrounds it. You may elect to pull the table from the text stream and treat it as a fixed element so text is forced to flow around it.

Tables are complex enough to warrant several chapters, or indeed a small book dedicated to the subject. The focus here is not to learn all that tables offer, but to focus on the use of tables in a complex document. We will briefly discuss how to create and modify a table, then spend the rest of the Chapter on topics that relate to their use in complex documents.

How to Insert a Predefined Table

Word maintains a gallery of Building Block tables which make their initial creation easy. You may also define a table for use that suits your needs and save it as a Building Block.

Step 1.   Position the insertion point where you wish to insert a table.

Step 2.   From the **Insert** tab, on the **Table** group, choose **Table**, then select **Quick Tables**. A gallery will appear and display built-in and custom table Building Blocks.

Step 3.   Select the desired table from the gallery.

How to Manually Create a Table

This procedure inserts a simple and unformatted table. Once inserted, you may select from a gallery of table styles if desired. Table styles were introduced beginning on page 48.

Step 1.   Position the insertion point where you wish to insert a table.

Step 2.   From the **Insert** tab, on the **Table** group, choose **Table**.

Step 3.   Use the mouse to drag over the grid in the **Insert** area to define a table graphically. As you move over the grid an indicator will display how many rows and columns you have selected. Click once to insert the table. If you require a larger table see the following note.

 If you require a table that exceeds the grid's 10 column by 8 row capacity, instead choose **Insert Table**. Use the spinner controls to adjust the number of rows and columns you need, then choose **OK**.

How to Create a Table by Drawing

This is actually a fun way to create a table, and is very useful if you need a table that would otherwise require merging cells since you are completely free to draw the table structure as you like (see the following illustration). By controlling where you draw horizontal and vertical lines you essentially establish the rows, columns, and individual cells.

Step 1.   Position the insertion point where you wish to insert a table.

Step 2.   From the **Insert** tab, on the **Table** group, choose **Table**, then select **Draw table**. The mouse pointer will switch to a pencil icon to indicate that you are in table drawing mode.

Step 3.   Use the mouse to draw a rectangle that represents the outer boundary of the table. This is done by positioning the mouse at either the top right or top left point of the future table, clicking and dragging a rectangle down and over. When the rectangle has been defined release the mouse. Word will insert the table and automatically activate the **Design** tab associated with **Table Tools.**

Step 4.   Use the mouse pointer to draw vertical (columns) or horizontal (rows) lines. Note that the behavior is that each line must begin and end at a line (no lines may be created that "hang" on one end. In reality you are creating individual cells in this manner. In the following illustration, the mouse pointer is being used to draw a line to vertically split the lower right cell in a table.

Step 5.   Continue drawing lines as needed. If you make a mistake, select the **Eraser** from the **Draw Borders** group on the **Design** tab and select the line to erase. To return to drawing select the **Draw Table** tool.

 A table created by drawing is identical in all other aspects to a table created from a gallery or using the **Insert Table** command.

Formatting Tables

We previously were introduced to Table Styles, including both the predefined styles and the ability to create and apply your own (refer to page 48). Here we will briefly discuss other methods of applying formatting to a table, or to a part of a table such as individual rows, columns, or cells. Part of formatting includes how the table relates to the text stream, so we will discuss placement options as well. Lastly, settings that control table behavior at a page break will be discussed. These topics have been chosen as they relate more directly to their use in a document intended for publication.

One important point is to maintain a consistent look among the tables in a large document. You may have a need to format two or more different styles, but keep differences to a minimum. Creating a table style or making consistent use of a predefined style is a good way to ensure uniform appearance.

How to Manually Format a Table

Formatting options for a table are generally applied to the selected element. If the insertion point is in an individual cell, formatting is applied only to that cell. To apply formatting to one or more rows or columns, first select those elements. To select the entire table, use the **table Selector**, which is a small square that will appear to the upper outer left corner of a table when the mouse floats over the table.

Step 1.   Select the desired element (or the entire table) to format.

Step 2.   Use the following table as a guide for formatting various aspects of the table.

Format	Procedure
Font attributes	Select the **Home** tab and use the controls in the **Font** or **Paragraph** group.
Shading/Borders	Move to the **Design** tab associated with **Table Tools**. Use the **Shading** and/or **Borders** controls, located in the **table Styles** group. To adjust border color, style, or weight use the controls associated with the **Draw Borders** group.
Text alignment	You can adjust horizontal alignment by using alignment controls associated with the **Paragraph** group on the **Home** tab, but for horizontal *and* vertical positioning use the controls associated with the **Alignment** group on the **Layout** tab of **Table Tools**.
Height or Width of cells	Use the **Cell Size** controls located on the **Layout** tab of **Table Tools**. Note that adjustments to cell height or width adjust row height or column width as well. To make an individual cell wider or taller than neighboring cells you may need to merge the cell with a neighboring cell.
Column or row properties	Select the table, then right click and select **Table Properties**, or from the **Layout** tab associated with **Table Tools**, in the **Table** group, choose **Properties**. Select either the **Row** or **Column** tab and make the desired adjustments.

How to Position a Table in the Text Stream

By default an inserted table occupies 100% of the available width (from left to right margin) and is embedded in the text stream. If text above the table is added or removed, the table will flow downward or upward, respectively, along with the rest of the text. You can position a table within the text stream or elect to pull it from the stream and force text to flow around it. The latter feature is typically used in Desktop Publishing.

Step 1.   Select the table of interest. Either right click on the table selector and choose **Table Properties** from the shortcut menu, or from the **Layout** tab associated with **Table Design**, in the **Table** group, choose **Properties**. The **Table Properties** dialog will appear similar to the following:

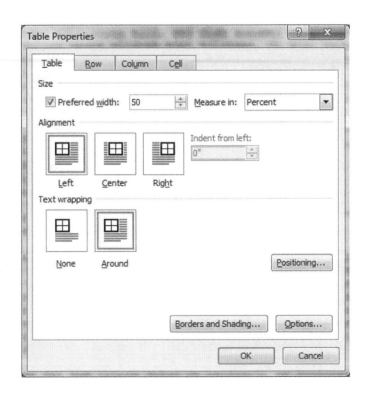

Option	Description
Size	Sets a preferred width, in physical dimensions such as cm or inches, or as a percent of the available width (the latter is the default).
Alignment	Aligns the table horizontally on the page. If the table is embedded in the text stream and is less than 100% of the available width, space to the left or right of the table is blank. Otherwise, if **Text wrapping** is set to **Around**, text will flow around the table.
Text wrapping	Determines whether the table is treated as an object as wide as the available width and flows with text, or whether text may flow around the table. The latter option defaults to the table still moving with text.
Positioning	For tables set to **Text wrapping - Around**, use this control to determine whether the table is anchored to a point on the page or whether it will flow with the text. If anchored, this option also provides choices for anchor points on the page to control vertical and/or horizontal position.
Borders and Shading	Opens the **Borders and Shading** dialog. This control offers many choices also available from the **Design** tab associated with **Table Tools**.
Options	Set default internal margins for cells (also known as *padding*), as well as set whether space is permitted between cells (also known as *gutters*).

Step 2.   Make the desired adjustments to the table, and choose **OK** when done.

How to Control Breaks in a Table

For tables that flow with the text stream, and for very large tables, Word's default behavior is to permit the table to be broken if it enters the area between pages. Although Word will try to keep the contents of a row together, the default behavior is to also permit the page break to appear *within* a row if necessary.

You basically have three options: (1) permit breaks across pages with or without permitting a row to break as well, (2) configure the table so it may not break across a page boundary—note that this will not work for very large tables, or (3) anchor the table on the page so it isn't affected by text flow. The latter option was discussed in the previous procedure. Note that one problem with anchoring arises if numerous or extensive edits to the document place too much distance between the text that refers to the table and the table itself.

How to Configure a Table for Page Breaks

Generally there are two settings you should think about if permitting a table to break across a page boundary. The first is whether the row or rows which may make up a table header repeat at the top of the broken table, and whether to permit a row to break *within* the row.

Step 1.   Move to the table of interest. To set one or more rows as repeating headers, select the row or rows that make up the header (they must be contiguous).

Step 2.   Move to the **Layout** tab associated with **Table Design**, and from the **Data** group, select **Repeat Header Rows**.

Step 3.   To control whether one or more rows may break at a page boundary, select the row or rows to control (they need not be contiguous).

Step 4.   From the **Layout** tab associated with **Table Tools**, in the **Table** area, select **Properties**.

Step 5.   On the **Table Properties** dialog box, select the **Row** tab, then enable or disable **Allow row to break across pages**.

How to Prevent a Table from Breaking

Oddly the **Table Properties** does not offer a solution to prevent a table from being split at a page boundary. **Allow row to break across pages** does not work as its effect is *within* each row, even if contiguous rows have this property set. To keep an entire table together you enforce the **Keep with next** property of paragraphs.

Step 1.   Select the desired table (alternatively, select all rows except the last one)

Step 2. Move to the **Home** tab, and select the **Dialog Expander** associated with the **Paragraph** group.

Step 3. On the **Paragraph** dialog box, select the **Line and Page Breaks** tab, then enable **Keep with next**. Close the dialog box.

Modifying Table Structure

A table may be modified by inserting, deleting or resizing rows or columns; inserting or deleting individual cells; or by merging two or more cells.

Resizing Table Elements

Rows and columns may be resized using graphical methods or by modifying properties. When you resize an individual cell it does affect the row or column that defines the cell. If you need to increase the size of a specific cell it may make sense to merge it with a neighboring cell.

How to Resize Columns Using the Mouse

When you resize a column, the default behavior is that the column to the right of the adjusted column is affected by the change (it either shrinks or widens). If you are adjusting the right-most column the table width changes. You can override this behavior as outlined below.

Step 1. To resize a column graphically, position the mouse pointer on the column's right boundary (if adjusting the right-most column, position the mouse over the table right boundary) until it becomes a left/right arrow.

Step 2. Use the following table as a guide to control the resizing behavior.

Key Action	Behavior
No keys used	As you drag the mouse pointer to the left or right, the target column and the column to its right (or table width if working with the last column) are affected. No other columns change width.
Shift + drag	As you adjust the width of the target column, no other column widths are affected. Rather, the entire *table* changes width by the same amount as the adjusted column.
Ctrl + drag	Adjusting the width of any column except the last one distributes the change over all columns to the right (whereas no key used only affects the column to the immediate right).
Alt + drag	The behavior is the same as no keys used (default), except the ruler changes to show the column width for each column in the table.

How to Resize Columns Using a Dialog Box

Step 1.   Select the table and open the **Table Properties** dialog box (see the previous procedures for details).

Step 2.   Select the **Column** tab.

Step 3.   Use the **Previous** or **Next** column control to select the desired column.

Step 4.   Set the **Preferred Width** for the column.

Step 5.   To work with additional rows, repeat Steps 3 and 4. Choose **OK** when done.

 To quickly resize two or more columns evenly, use the mouse to select two or more contiguous columns. With the mouse point still appearing as a black downward-pointing arrow, right click and choose **Distribute columns evenly**.

How to Resize a Row Using the Mouse

Row resizing does not affect other rows as column resizing does. When you increase or decrease the height or one or more rows, it affects overall table height only.

Step 1.   To resize a row graphically, position the mouse pointer over the bottom border of the target row. When the mouse pointer becomes an up/down arrow, click and drag up or down to adjust row height.

How to Resize a Row Using a Dialog Box

Step 1.   Select the table and open the **Table Properties** dialog box (see the previous procedures for details).

Step 2.   Select the **Row** tab.

Step 3.   Use the **Previous** or **Next** row control to select the desired row.

Step 4.   Set the **Specified Height** for the row. The options for **Row height is** are *At least* to set a minimum height (the row height can increase depending upon content), or *Exactly* (content may be clipped if it cannot fit within the allotted height). Choose **OK** when done.

 To quickly resize two or more rows evenly, use the mouse to select two or more contiguous rows. With the mouse point still appearing as a white upward/right-pointing arrow, right click and choose **Distribute rows evenly**.

Inserting and Deleting Table Elements

Inserting a row or a column in a table is straightforward—you can elect to insert the new row or column in relation to the currently-selected row or column. When you delete a row or column the table adjusts and any content in the deleted row or column is also deleted. When you insert or delete one or more cells it can affect table structure in odd ways, as will be illustrated.

How to Insert a Row or Column

The quickest method is to use the mouse.

Step 1.   Use the mouse to select a row or column that will neighbor the inserted row or column.

Step 2.   In Word 2007/2010, right click and from the shortcut menu, choose either **Insert Rows Above**, **Insert Rows Below**, **Insert Columns to the Right**, or **Insert Columns to the left**. In Word 2013 position the mouse close to the row or column boundary you wish to modify. When an insertion tool appears, click on the **+** button.

 If you select two or more rows or columns and follow this procedure, Word will insert as many rows or columns as you have selected, otherwise the default is to insert a single row or column.

To insert a row or column using command buttons:

Step 1.   Use the mouse to select a row or column that will end up adjacent to the inserted row or column.

Step 2.   From the **Rows & Columns** group on the **Layout** tab associated with the **Table Design**, select the desired action.

 You may also add an additional row by positioning the insertion point in the lowest right cell and pressing *Tab*.

How to Delete a Row or Column

Again, using the mouse is the quickest method.

Step 1.   Use the mouse to select the desired row, rows, column, or columns to delete.

Step 2.   Right click while still in row- or column-selection mode and choose either **Delete rows** or **Delete columns**.

To delete a row or column using command buttons:

Step 1.   Use the mouse to select a row or column that will end up adjacent to the inserted row or column.

Step 2.   From the **Rows & Columns** group on the **Layout** tab associated with the **Table Design**, choose **Delete**, then select the specific action from the menu.

 Deleting rows decreases the overall table height by shifting any downstream rows upward. Deleting columns decreases the width of the table by shifting any right-ward columns to the left. Any content contained within the deleted row or column is also deleted.

How to Insert or Delete Cells

This option has the odd effect of potentially changing the table structure. When you insert a cell within a table, Word offers four actions: **Shift Cells Right**, **Shift Cells Down**, **Insert Entire Row** or **Insert Entire Column**. Only the first two choices actually insert an individual cell.

When one or more cells are deleted, Word offers similar options: **Shift Cells Left**, **Shift Cells Up**, **Delete Entire Row**, or **Delete Entire Column**.

The effect of selecting and deleting two cells, and choosing **Shift Cells Left** is illustrated below:

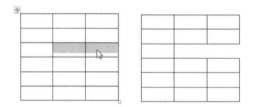

To insert additional cells:

Step 1.   Select the cell at the location in the table where you wish to insert an additional cell.

Step 2.   Right click and from the shortcut menu, choose **Insert**, then **Cells**.

Step 3.   Select the desired option. If you choose **Shift cells right**, one or more cells will be thrust rightward beyond the current table right boundary. Choosing **Shift cells down** typically inserts a full row.

To delete a cell or cells

Step 1.   Select the cell or cells to delete. They must be contiguous if deleting multiple cells.

Step 2.   Right click and from the shortcut menu, choose **Delete**, then **Cells**.

Step 3.   Select the desired option. If you choose **Shift cells up**, only the content of any cells below the current location will move upward. If you choose **Shift cells left**, the table will be modified in a manner similar to that illustrated above.

Merging or Splitting Cells

A far less disruptive operation is to merge two or more cells, or to split an individual cell. In both cases the overall table structure is unaffected. When you merge cells that contain content, the content is merged as well. Splitting a cell with content locates the content into the upper right-most cell after the split. The following illustration shows a table before and after a merge and split operation. The cell containing the content *Two* was split into 2 columns and 2 rows, while the cells containing the content *Three* and *Four* were merged.

One	Two	Three	Four

One	Two		Three
			Four

How to Split a Cell

Step 1.   Position the mouse in the cell to split, or select two or more contiguous cells to split. Either right-click and choose **Split cells** or from the **Layout** tab, in the **Merge** group, choose **Split Cells**.

Step 2.   In the **Split Cells** dialog box, select the number of columns and/or rows to add. If you selected two or more cells, indicate whether to merge cell content prior to splitting. If you choose not to merge, the content of any cell to the right and/or below the top-left selected cell will be discarded. Choose **OK** to split the cell(s).

How to Merge Cells

Step 1.   Select the two or more cells to merge.

Step 2.   Right click and from the shortcut menu select **Merge Cells**, or from the **Layout** tab in the **Merge** group, choose **Merge Cells**.

Splitting a Table

Splitting a table has two effects, depending upon the location of the insertion point. If the insertion point is anywhere in the table except the first row the table will split above the insertion point location. If the insertion point is in the top row, splitting the table simply places a paragraph mark above the table. The latter is sometimes used by authors when confronted by a table that begins at the absolute top of a document. Another way to insert a paragraph mark above a table is to position the insertion point in the top right cell, before any content, and press *Enter*.

How to Split a Table

Step 1.   Position the insertion point in the row immediately below the split point.

Step 2.   From the **Layout** tab associated with **Table Design**, in the **Merge** group, choose **Split Table**.

Referencing Tables

Tables are one of the objects which can be *captioned*, and in doing so you can either create an entry for each captioned table in a document's table of contents, or you may create a separate table of tables (these specifics will be addressed in Chapter 8). When you create a caption, text that auto increments by table number is assigned the *Caption* style. A caption will appear above or below the table (you may also move the caption to within the table structure).

If additional tables are inserted upstream, all tables downstream automatically adjust their caption number. Word internally numbers all tables in a document, but only captioned tables are accounted for in the caption auto number, thus ensuring that the caption numbers are consistent and increment correctly.

How to Caption a Table

Step 1.   Position the insertion point in the table to caption.

Step 2.   On the **References** tab, in the **Captions** group, select **Insert Caption**. The **Caption** dialog box will appear similar to the following:

Option	Description
Caption	Used to create the caption and any text you desire. To add text to the caption, position the insertion point to the right of the auto number and type.
Label	Select from a choice of caption labels. Other options are *Figure, Equation, Exhibit,* and *Graph*. If you need a custom label, use the **New Label** command (see below).
Position	Position the caption either above or below the table. If this option is disabled, it is because the insertion point was above or below the table and not within the table. In this case Word assumes you want the caption at the insertion point location.
Exclude label from caption	When selected, will omit the word *Table* from the caption. The auto number will still appear in the caption.
New Label...	Use to create a custom label. Any custom label you create is stored in **normal.dotx** (you cannot change the storage location).
Delete Label	Removes the selected label type from **normal.dotx**.
Numbering	Selects the numbering style (the same as those options for page numbering). For example, *1, 2, 3*, or *A, B, C*. If you are using complex chapter and page numbering (see page 87) you may choose to include the chapter number along with the table number.
AutoCaption...	Establishes automatic captioning. A caption will automatically appear for each table you insert into a document.

Step 3.   Create a caption for the table and adjust settings to suite your needs. Choose **OK** when done.

The shortcut to opening the **Caption** dialog box is to right click on the **Table Selector** and choose **Insert Caption** from the shortcut menu.

Chapter 7 | Working with Graphics

Graphics include a broad variety of elements that share a common feature in the way they may interact with the text stream. In its simplest form, a graphic element is an object that may be embedded within the text stream (in which case Word basically treats the graphic as a large character) or it may be configured so it is apart from the text stream. In the latter case, the graphic may be set to flow in the stream or be anchored to a point on a page. We first saw this behavior with tables. Graphics differ from tables set apart from the text stream in that *wrap points* may be used with graphics to create sophisticated edges between graphic and text.

As with tables, any graphic element may be captioned. This action opens the way for inclusion into a table of contents, or for the creation of a separate table of figures, charts, equations, etc.

This chapter cannot be a full treatment on graphics, and thus we'll assume you have publication-ready images on hand. We will discuss on a casual level some formatting of images as they relate to word processing. Likewise, we will not extensively tour the various clip art and shapes that Word makes available, although the general procedure to embed these objects will be covered. Lastly, we will discuss embedding objects from other applications such as Microsoft Excel tables and/or graphs, and slides from PowerPoint presentations. At one level, these objects are included simply because they are treated similarly to other graphics. As objects "owned" by other applications, we will also discuss how to embed and link these objects. This powerful technique means, for example, that a table embedded from an Excel worksheet may be edited by others, working in Microsoft Excel, and those changes are automatically updated in the embedded image in a Word document.

Graphics Basics

We alluded to the fact that several types of objects—digital images, clipart and shapes, text boxes, embedded Excel worksheets or charts, PowerPoint slides, and equations—are all considered as graphic elements due to how they are managed from within Microsoft Word. These elements all share a common core of attributes:

- A graphic may be embedded in the text stream, contained within a device that forces text to flow around it, or "lifted" above or "pushed" below the text layer.

- These elements may be resized, rotated, shaded, framed, and manipulated using a suite of graphics tools.

- Image files or objects from other applications (such as Microsoft Excel or PowerPoint) may be inserted or *linked*. The latter option means that any edits to the object, conducted in its parent application, are updated in the Word document. Thus, you may embed and link a graphic image that an illustrator is still working on. Any changes to the graphic, using a graphic manipulation program, are updated in the Word document.

- Graphic elements may be captioned in the same manner that tables are (discussed in the last Chapter). The built-in caption labels include *Figure, Exhibit, Graph*, and *Equation*. You may create additional, custom caption labels as well. As with tables, once captioned, you may refer to these elements in a table of contents, or create specific tables such as a table of figures or a table of equations.

Inserting Graphics

Word maintains three separate layers in a document (these three layers are also found in the header and footer area—making for a total of six layers); the main layer is where text is located while the other two layers are reserved for graphics (or text contained within a text box) and appear to float over or beneath the text layer. Thus, when you place a graphic element within a document, you choose which of these layers to use. When you use default values, the graphic is located *within* the text layer and as previously mentioned, is treated like a large character in the text stream.

We will first introduce inserting graphics using the default method, thus placing them within the text stream. The following section will discuss other placement options.

How to Insert a Graphic Element

Like all other objects, you begin by positioning the insertion point where you wish to insert the graphic. The following table lists, by object type, the overall procedure:

Object Type	Method
Digital Image File	From the **Insert** tab, in the **Illustrations** group, choose **Picture**. If you wish to link the image rather than embed it, select the desired option from the **Insert** button on the **Insert Image** dialog box. The table following this one outlines the options.
Clip Art	From the **Insert** tab, in the **Illustrations** group, choose **Clip Art**. Use the **Clip Art** pane to search for the desired artwork.
Shapes / Smart Art	From the **Insert** tab, in the **Illustrations** group, choose **Shapes** (or) **Smart Art**. Both elements are predefined shapes, the latter being useful for organization charts and other business-related purposes. Smart Art is highly formatted and is best used for presentation purposes or full color printing.
Text Box	From the **Insert** tab, in the **Text** group, choose **Text Box**, then select the desired text box from the gallery. To manually create a text box, choose **Draw Text Box** and use the mouse to create a rectangular text area.
Excel or PowerPoint Object	Discussed beginning on page 137.
Equation	Discussed beginning on page 142.

Image Insert Options

Option	Description
Insert	The image is imported into the Word document. If the original file is modified the image in Word is not updated, so you must manually delete the inserted image and reinsert the updated version.
Link to File	The image appears in the Word document but is actually a reference to the image file. You may manually update the linked image using the **Links** dialog box (see page 141).
Insert and Link	In this option the image is both embedded in Word *and* linked to the original file. Update the image by using the **Links** dialog box (see page 141).

When you insert a graphic of any type, the default is to place the inserted object within the text stream. In the following before-and-after illustration, a graphic image is inserted to the immediate left of the highlighted text. Note that Word adjusts the height of the text line containing the inserted image and that text downstream of the insert point is pushed downward.

Text Flow and Graphics

The default placement for an inserted graphic element is within the text stream. For many documents (including this book) this arrangement works fine. When an inserted element is treated like a paragraph the graphic may be aligned or centered using standard paragraph formatting attributes. However, there are circumstances when it is desirable to create text flow around the graphic.

Any graphic element may be configured so that text flows around it. In the previous illustration, note how the line containing the inserted graphic expanded to accommodate its height. In the following illustration, the same graphic has been configured so text flows around it. Note the small anchor icon to the far left— that indicates that the image is anchored to a point on the page.

The following table highlights the options available when you move an inserted graphic out of the text layer:

Text Wrapping Options

Option	Description
Square	Word wraps text around the square container of the image.
Tight	If possible, Word determines if text can bleed over the image container for a tighter text flow. This can be manually manipulated using **Wrap Points**.
Behind/In front of Text	The image is moved to the layer either below or above the text layer plane. In the former case the text will flow over the image while in the latter case the image will obscure any text underneath of it. **Opacity** is a property of images which can be adjusted to make interesting effects when using either graphics layer.
Top and bottom	Word forces text to flow past the graphic but not to the right or left of it. The visual appearance is similar to a graphic inserted in line with text, although this option permits text to flow past the graphic.
Through	Similar to **Tight**, but the effect depends upon whether Word can determine if sufficient white space exists surrounding the graphic to use as a text flow area.
In line with text	This is the default behavior. The graphic is treated in line with the surrounding text. There is no text flow using this option.

How to Specify Text Flow

The procedure depends upon whether the object is an image or some other graphic object (such as clip art or an inserted object from Excel or PowerPoint).

Step 1.   Select the object by clicking once on it. A series of selection handles should appear, indicating that Word has placed the object in a selection mode.

Step 2.   Choose text flow options using one of the following techniques:

Starting Point	Procedure
Page Layout Tab	From the **Arrange** group, choose **Text Wrapping**, then select from the gallery of options or select **More layout options…**
Picture Tools, Layout Tab	In the **Arrange** group, choose **Text Wrapping** as above.
Shortcut Menu	Right click on the graphic. If working with an image select **Text Wrapping**, then proceed as above. If working with an object, select **Format AutoShape**, or **Format Object**. From the **Format AutoShape** or **Format Object** dialog box, move to the **Text Wrapping** tab and select **Advanced**.
Layout Options	In Word 2013, a **Layout Options** menu floats to the upper right corner of the graphic. Select it and choose from the list or select **See more** to open the **Advanced Layout** dialog.

Step 3.   Select the desired text layout option. If you choose **More layout options**, or **Format Object/AutoShape**, the **Text Wrapping** tab of the **Advanced Layout** dialog box will appear similar to the following:

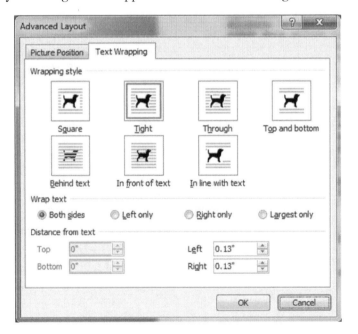

Option	Description
Wrapping Style	Displays all text wrapping options, with the current scheme highlighted.
Wrap text	When text is permitted to wrap you can specify how it flows relative to the left and right side of the graphic.
Distance from text	Sets the gutters for the top, bottom, right, and left sides of the image. Note that only the gutters which have context for the current text wrapping style will be enabled.

Step 4.   Make adjustments to the text wrapping properties. Choose **OK** when done.

How to Control Graphic Position

You can control to a high degree of accuracy where a graphic appears on the page, setting horizontal, vertical, or both horizontal and vertical attributes. To begin this procedure, follow Steps 1-3 from the previous procedure so the **Advanced Layout** dialog box is open.

Step 1.   Select the **Picture Position** tab on the **Advanced Layout** dialog box. When selected, the tab will appear similar to the following:

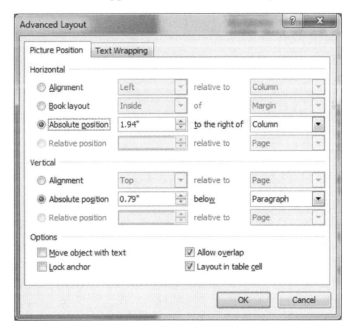

Option	Description
Horizontal	There are up to four options for positioning a graphic or text box horizontally on a page. The following table details these options.
Vertical	Vertical placement may be set using one of three options. These options are described in the following table.
Move object with text	If checked, the object will flow with the text stream. Locally, text will still flow around the object if the appropriate text flow option is chosen.
Lock anchor	When enabled, forces the object and its anchor to remain together. This is useful when you have a picture anchored to a paragraph that references it. By locking the anchor the image will always remain within sight of the referencing paragraph.
Allow overlap	Allows two objects of the same text flow settings to overlap if closely positioned.
Layout in table cell	For a graphic object positioned in a table cell, checking this option forces the graphic to remain within the cell. When unchecked (and if the appropriate text flow option is selected) the graphic can be positioned partially or fully outside the containing table cell.

Horizontal and Vertical Position Options

Option	Description
Horizontal Alignment	Aligns left, right, or center relative to a number of elements on the page, including the physical page, left or right margins, a column or individual character.
Horizontal Book Layout	Used only for publications where the left and right margin are different and are mirrored between odd and even pages. You can align relative to the margin (graphic is positioned close to the margin) or the page (graphic appears at extreme edge). When positioned *inside* elements are located to the left on odd paged and to the right on even pages. When positioned *outside* the opposite takes effect.
Horizontal Absolute	Sets an exact horizontal position, relative to an object you select (they are the same as the options for **Horizontal Alignment**). The positioning is to the right of the selected reference point, but you may specify negative values to nudge the graphic to the left.
Horizontal Relative	Specifies a horizontal position which is expressed as a percentage relative to the size of the selected reference point. This is useful for translating the document to a format such as HTML where the document may be viewed in a variety of screen widths.
Vertical Alignment	Similar to **Horizontal Alignment** except there are more position options and some of the relative reference points, such as *line* reflect the nature of moving vertically in a document.
Vertical Absolute	Similar to **Horizontal Absolute** except the reference points reflect objects such as *line*.
Vertical Relative	Similar to **Horizontal Relative** above.

Step 2.   Make any changes to the positioning properties of your graphic. Choose **OK** when done.

Using Wrap Points to Control Text Wrapping

Once a graphic has been configured for text wrapping, Word establishes a set of *wrap points* that can be manipulated to control text flow. Wrap points define a border around a graphic element that controls text flow. By moving one or more of these wrap points, you can customize text flow around an object. For graphic images you import as a graphic file, Word adds four wrap points—one for each corner. Clip Art and shapes may have many more wrap points.

The following illustration shows, left to right, an embedded graphic image (the original is a JPEG file), the original configuration of wrap points, and a configuration where wrap points were manipulated. Note how the text flow responds to the modified wrap points.

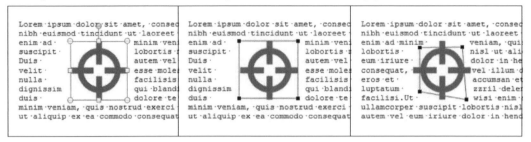

Wrapping becomes even more sophisticated when you work with a clip art or shape from one of Microsoft's galleries, as illustrated below.

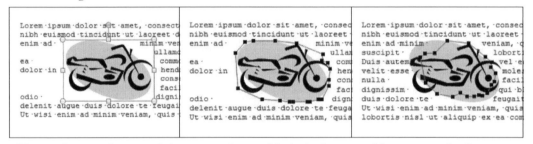

Wrap points may be moved closer onto the graphic (as in the case of the motorcycle clip art above, or farther away (as in the case of the crosshairs) in order to pull text closer or push text away from part of the graphic.

Wrap points are only available when the graphic's text wrapping attribute is set to *tight*.

How to Use Wrap Points

Step 1.   Select the desired graphic.

Step 2.   From the **Picture Tools | Format** tab, in the **Arrange** group, use the **Text Wrapping** control to ensure that text wrapping is set to *Tight*.

Step 3.   Return to the **Text Wrapping** control and choose **Edit wrap points**. Alternatively right-click on the graphic and select **Text wrapping**, then choose **Edit wrap points**. The graphic outline will change to a series or 4 or more wrap points as illustrated above. The line connecting wrap points is red.

Step 4.   Use the mouse to move individual wrap points as desired. The text flow will change as each point is moved.

Step 5.   To exit working with wrap points, click anywhere on the text layer, away from
           the graphic.

Manipulating Graphics

Microsoft Word offers a suite of tools to manipulate graphic elements. For simple tasks such as image resizing or rotation, these tools work well for all graphic element types. If you are working with an imported graphic file, you may achieve better results by making changes using a specific image manipulation program (all of the images for this book were manipulated using GIMP, an open source, full featured image manipulation program) and inserting the manipulated image. The images Microsoft provides, such as clip art and shapes, lend themselves well to being manipulated with the tools Word offers. The distinction is that a graphics file is more complex than the simpler clip art and shape images.

A Tour of the Picture Format Tab

When you select a graphic image, Word activates the **Format** tab associated with **Picture Tools**. The table below outlines the major groups associated with this tab.

Gallery	Description
Adjust	Control attributes of the image such as brightness, contrast, color, and compression options.
Picture Styles	A gallery of image border styles as well as controls to set border width and color; change picture shape; or apply special effects such as 3D, shadowing, etc. There is a Dialog Expander associated with this group that opens the **Format Picture** dialog box.
Arrange	Set text wrapping, positioning, z-order (the layer below or above the text layer); align two or more selected graphics; and rotate the image. In Word 2013 an additional tool, **Selection Pane** is available and lists all of the objects when your graphic (or selection) consists of multiple items.
Size	Crop or resize an image. This group has a Dialog Expander which opens the **Size** dialog box.

Many of the available picture tools apply predefined styles, either to the image border or to the image and/or its background. Like the old addage concerning fonts and desktop publishing (just because you can apply 45 fonts to a document doesn't mean you should!), take care when working with many of these features. You can end up creating a document where the imagery excessively pulls the reader's attention from the text. That said, we will review some of the tamed tools such as resizing or rotating an image.

Resizing a Graphic

Resizing clip art or a built-in shape is a safe operation as these image types were originally designed to resize seamlessly. Take care when resizing graphic files however. Changing the size of a graphic image involves applying an algorithm to discard (resize smaller) or intercalate (resize larger) pixels. Most professional-grade image manipulation programs use more sophisticated algorithms for this purpose, so you may consider resizing a graphic file in a dedicated application.

When you resize a graphic you are either resizing proportionately in order to maintain the overall aspect ratio of height to width, or you distort the image by resizing only in the horizontal or vertical direction.

How to Resize a Graphic Using the Mouse

Step 1.   Select the graphic to be resized. The graphic will appear with selection handles as illustrated below:

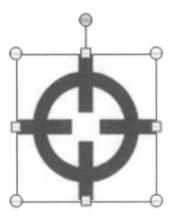

Step 2.   To proportionately resize the graphic, grab one of the round selection points located at one of the corners of the graphic. Click to drag inward (resize smaller), or outward (resize larger). Release the mouse when the desired size is achieved.

Step 3.   To distort the image, grab one of the square selection points, located at the mid points of the selection rectangle. To compress or enlarge the graphic horizontally, select the left or right-hand square and drag inward or outward, respectively. To compress or enlarge the image vertically, use the top or bottom square selection point. Release the mouse when done.

How to Resize a Graphic Using a Dialog Box

You gain a bit more control over resizing when using this method over the mouse-based approach.

Step 1.   Select the graphic to be resized.

Step 2.   On the **Format** tab associated with **Picture Tools**, in the **Size** area, select the **Dialog Expander**. The **Size** dialog box will appear as follows:

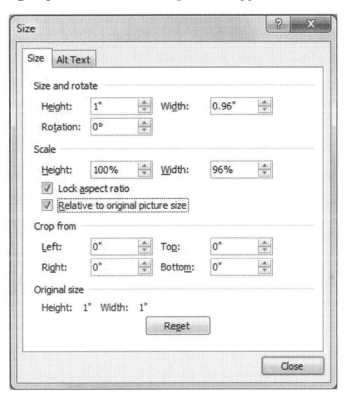

Option	Description
Size and rotate	Display or set the physical height and/or width of the graphic. Rotate the graphic 360° in 1° increments.
Scale	Scale the image as a percent of either the original (if **Relative to original picture size** is checked), or to the current size of the image when selected. If **Lock aspect ratio** is selected, the image resizes proportionately, otherwise changes distort the image horizontally or vertically.
Crop from	Crops the image by moving the image border. Positive numbers move the border inward, negative numbers move it outward. Discussed in the following section.
Original Size	Displays the original image physical dimensions.

Step 3.   Make changes to the image size properties as desired. Use **OK** when done.

Rotating a Graphic

Again, there are two methods for image rotation. Use of the mouse or via a more finely-tuned dialog box. Use the mouse for casual rotation adjustments and the dialog box when you need to rotate the graphic by an exact amount.

How to Rotate a Graphic Using the Mouse

Step 1.   Select the image to rotate. The graphic will appear with selection handles as previously illustrated.

Step 2.   Use the mouse to select the green rotation control, located at the top of the selection square. Move the mouse to the right or left to rotate the image. While a rotation operation is in effect the mouse pointer will change to a rotation symbol as illustrated:

Step 3   Release the mouse when finished.

How to Rotate a Graphic Using a Dialog Box

Step 1.   Follow the first two steps in the procedure **How to Resize a Graphic using a Dialog Box**.

Step 2.   Adjust the rotation using the **Rotation** control. Negative rotation will convert to values greater than 180°.

Cropping a Graphic

Cropping refers to adjustments to the edge of the container housing the graphic element. Like moving a shutter over the graphic, this crop line trims the image. Moving a crop line is not the same as resizing, although manipulating the edge using the mouse is a similar technique. As with the previous procedures, you can use either the mouse or a dialog box to crop.

How to Crop a Graphic using the Mouse

Step 1.   Select the graphic to crop.

Step 2.   From the **Format** tab associated with **Picture Tools**, in the **Size** group, choose **Crop**. The image will appear contained within a cropping selection as illustrated below.

Step 3.   Select one of the 8 cropping handles. The corner handles will crop both horizontally and vertically while the mid-point handles only crop the appropriate edge. You decrease the image size by drawing a cropping margin inward, and increase the graphic size by drawing outward. In the latter case, white space is added to the graphic.

How to Crop a Graphic Using a Dialog Box

Step 1.   Follow the first two steps in the procedure **How to Resize a Graphic using a Dialog Box**.

Step 2.   Use the **Crop from** controls to adjust cropping. To crop diagonally you use the two controls that together correspond to the corner of interest. As you make adjustments the graphic changes to display the effect.

Inserting Objects

An object, which in this context is taken to mean a unit of presentation material created and managed by another application, is treated like any other graphic element in Microsoft Word. They are discussed separately as the methods of inserting, updating, and managing them are different from standard graphics such as image files or clip art.

We introduced the concept of linking a graphic file early in this Chapter. Linking applies to objects as well and is a powerful tool for keeping the data in a document up to date. You may elect to embed and link an object, or simply embed it. If you do not link, any changes to the object back in its parent application are not updated in the Word document. When linked, any changes made by you or others to the original data are updated in Word.

There are several ways to place an object in a Word document. We will tour each of these and then discuss how to update linked objects. The most popular objects to work with are Microsoft Excel worksheets and charts, and slides from a PowerPoint presentation. We will focus on working with these objects but any Windows application that supports OLE (object linking and embedding), or Automation, will offer this functionality as well. See the note at the end of the procedure which begins on page 139.

Inserting an Object as a File

When you insert an object by referencing its file, what gets inserted depends upon the application. For example, when inserting a PowerPoint slide show containing multiple slides, only the first slide is inserted. In Excel, only a single worksheet is inserted although which worksheet depends on which one had the focus when the workbook file was saved! To control with certainty which object is inserted, follow the procedure using the clipboard.

Step 1.   Position the insertion point in the document where the object will be placed.

Step 2.   From the **Insert** tab, in the **Text** area, choose **Object**.

Step 3.   On the **Object** dialog box, select the **Create from file** tab.

Step 4.   Use the **Browse** button and locate the file to insert. Choose the **Insert** button.

Step 5.   Back on the **Object** dialog, select **Link to file** to enable automatic linking.

Step 6.   Choose **OK**.

 The other option on the **Object** dialog is **Display as Icon**. This is not recommended as only an icon representing the parent application, and not the actual data, is displayed. You must double click on the icon to view the data (which opens in the parent application).

Inserting an Object as a New Object

This procedure creates a new object in its parent container. When object creation is complete, you can save it as a file in the parent application, then return to Word. The object you created is then inserted into your document. We will follow an example of creating a small table in Microsoft Excel.

Step 1.   Follow the first two steps from the previous procedure.

Step 2.   Ensure that the **Create New** tab is selected on the **Object** dialog. Scroll through the list of OLE/Automation applications. In this example, we will select **Microsoft Office Excel Worksheet**. Choose **OK**. A small window will open, reflecting a portion of an Excel worksheet (see the following illustration). The standard ribbons in Word will change to reflect Microsoft Excel ribbons.

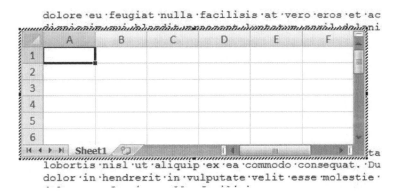

Step 3.   Use the Workbook object, as well as any Excel commands and functions available from the tab area, to create new content.

Step 4.   To return to Microsoft Word, click away from the Excel object window and on the underlying document. The Excel table will appear in the text as follows:

blandit·praesent·luptatum·zzril·delenit·augue·duis
facilisi.¶

Number of Latin Speakers by Country by Year				
	Italy	Spain	France	England
Year				
1400	560,000	1,345,000	3,250,750	2,550,600
1800	375,000	875,000	1,870,000	1,340,500
2000	8,700	1,560	4,550	12,500

d·minim·veniam,·quis·nostrud·exerci·tation·ullamco
ut·aliquip·ex·ea·commodo·consequat.·Duis·autem·vel

The list of applications referred to in Step 2 of the previous procedure are all registered with Microsoft Windows as supporting OLE/Automation. Data from any of these applications may be inserted as an embedded object within a Word document and updated using the procedures discussed beginning on page 141.

Inserting an Object Using the Clipboard

The most useful method for controlling what information appears in a document is to use the Windows Clipboard. You first open the application that contains the data to insert and select the desired portion. For example, you can select a portion of a larger table in an Excel workbook, an entire Excel chart, or the contents of a single slide in a PowerPoint presentation. Once the selection has been copied to the clipboard, you return to Word and paste it into your document.

Step 1.   Open the application that manages the target data. For example, open Microsoft Excel to select and insert a section of a worksheet or an Excel graph.

Step 2.   Select the data. For example, select a section of a worksheet, a graph, or a slide from a PowerPoint slideshow. Press **Ctrl C** to copy the selection.

Step 3.   Close the application, if desired. Return to Microsoft Word and position the insertion point in the document where you wish to insert the data.

Step 4.   Press **Ctrl V**, or for more control over the nature of the insertion, from the **Home** tab, on the **Clipboard** group, choose **Paste** and then select **Paste Special**. The **Paste Special** dialog box will appear as illustrated:

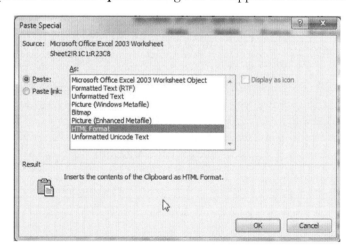

Step 5.   Select the desired format from the **As** list box. If you wish to link the inserted object, select **Paste link**.

Step 6.   Choose **OK**.

The list of paste options in **Paste Special** will vary depending upon the content type and the parent application.

The content choice that is selected when you open **Paste Special** is the type that would be used if you had simply pasted the content in Step 4.

Updating Linked Objects

There are two broad methods of updating a link. Double clicking on a linked object will open the parent application and load the linked data. Using the **Links** dialog you can control the nature of updating. The former method is best if you are the owner of the linked data and need to make a change. Use the second method if others own or edit the linked data and your responsibility is to ensure that the document stays up to date.

How to Update Linked Data Using the Mouse

Step 1.   Double click on the linked object. The object will open in its parent application.

Step 2.   Make any edits as needed.

Step 3.   Return to Microsoft Word by clicking once on the underlying text, away from the linked object.

How to Update Linked Data Using the Links Manager (2007)

Step 1.   Click once on the **Office Button**.

Step 2.   Choose **Prepare**, then select **Edit links to files**. The **Links** dialog box will appear similar to the following:

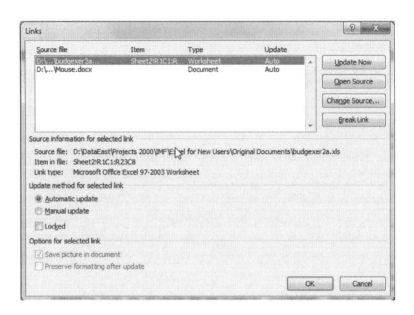

Option	Description
Source File	Lists the linked objects along with properties for each link.
Update method for selected link	Choose *Automatic Update* to permit Word to update the links or *Manual Update* if you want to control when a link is updated. If you select the latter option you will need to use the **Links** dialog box to conduct any updates.
Options for selected link	If the selected link is a linked graphic file, **Save picture in document** ensures that the picture, and not an icon of the parent application, is displayed. If an embedded picture is formatted in Word, checking **Preserve formatting after update** maintains the applied formatting when the image is updated.
Update Now	Forces the selected link to be updated.
Open Source	Opens the selected link in its parent application.
Change Source	Change the source for the selected link.
Break Link	Removes the selected link. This *does not* remove the object.

How to Update Linked Data Using the Links Manager (2010/2013)

You must save a document that contains linked objects before you can use the **Links** manager.

Step 1.   Select the **File** tab, then choose **Info**.

Step 2.   In the **Related Documents** area, choose **Edit links to files**. The **Links** Manager will appear. Use the figure and table from the previous procedure as a guide.

 In Word 2013 you may also right click on any linked object and select **Linked (object type) Object**, then choose **Edit links**.

Equations

Equations are created in Word using an equation editor. They are generally treated like other graphic elements with the exception that in order to fully control text flow you should insert the equation into a **Text Box**. Resizing an equation is a matter of font size since equations behave like a collection of characters and symbols.

Word can display equations in one of three modes: in line as part of the character stream, isolated from the text as an independent paragraph, or contained within a text box. In in-line mode, Word will reduce the size of the equation automatically. When treated as an independent paragraph or contained within a text box, Word will display the equation in its normal size.

How to Insert an Equation into the Text Stream

In this procedure, the equation is inserted directly into the document. In most academic endeavors equations are separated from the text by isolating them as separate paragraphs. This is the recommended procedure to follow. If you have additional formatting requirements, consider the next procedure where a text box is used as the container.

Step 1.   Position the insertion point in the document where you wish to insert an equation. For most purposes, this should be a blank paragraph.

Step 2.   From the **Insert** tab in the **Symbols** group, choose **Equation**. Select from the gallery of predefined equations or choose **Insert new equation** to create a custom equation. An example of an inserted equation appears below.

mmy ·nibh ·euismod ·tincidunt ·ut ·laoreet ·do

$$f(x) = a_0 + \sum_{n=1}^{\infty} \left(a_n \cos\frac{n\pi x}{L} + b_n \sin\frac{n\pi x}{L} \right)$$

iriure ·dolor ·in ·hendrerit ·in ·vulputate ·v
m ·dolore ·eu ·feugiat ·nulla ·facilisis ·at ·v

Step 3.   If desired, make adjustments to the equation by selecting the right-hand drop down arrow. Choose from the following options:

Option	Description
Save as new equation	Saves the equation as a building block.
Professional	Arranges the equation on one or more lines, depending upon the equation. In the illustration above, the equation is presented in **Professional** layout.
Linear	Forces the equation to adopt a single line.
Change to inline	Forces the equation to display in-line with any text, or if isolated as a paragraph, flush left.
Change to display	Places the equation on its own paragraph, centered.
Justification	When displayed rather than inline, these options set justification.

Step 4.   Make adjustments as desired. To exit the equation editor, click on any text on the document.

How to Insert an Equation into a Text Box

By placing an equation in a text box, you gain all of the image manipulation features attributed to text boxes. For example, by placing the text box in the text stream as **Tight**, you can use Wrap Points to customize how text flows around the equation. Resizing the text box will not resize the equation.

Step 1.   Position the insertion point in the document.

Step 2.   From the **Insert** tab, on the **Text** group, choose **Text Box**. From the gallery select a predefined text box or select **Draw Text Box** to manually create one.

Step 3.   Make any adjustments to the text box, such as text flow or position.

Step 4.   Place the insertion point *inside* the text box.

Step 5.   Proceed with the procedure above, beginning with Step 2.

Referencing Graphics

Graphics, like tables, are objects which can be *captioned* and in doing so you can either create an entry for each captioned table in a document's table of contents, or you may create a separate table of figures, table of equations, etc. (creating such tables will be addressed in Chapter 8). When you create a caption, text that auto increments by graphic number (as determined by the ordinal number beginning with the first graphic in the document) is assigned the *Caption* style. The caption will appear above or below the graphic.

If additional graphics of a given type are inserted upstream, all captions downstream automatically adjust their caption number. Word internally numbers all captions by type in a document, but only captioned graphics are accounted for in the caption auto number, thus ensuring that the caption numbers are consistent and increment correctly.

How to Caption a Graphic

Step 1.   Position the insertion point on the graphic to caption.

Step 2.   On the **References** tab, in the **Captions** group, select **Insert Caption**. See page 120 for details concerning the **Insert Caption** dialog box.

Step 3.   Create a caption for the graphic and adjust settings to suite your needs. Choose **OK** when done.

Word 2013 offers a shortcut for captions. Select the image and right click on it, then choose **Insert caption** from the shortcut menu.

Chapter 8 | References

The term *references* refers to a collection of document objects which share the trait of pointing to another location within a document. A table of contents references chapter or section headings, and usually also includes subheadings within each chapter or section. Likewise, a table of figures references each captioned figure within a document (we discussed this on page 145). A cross reference points to text or a page number where a specific item appears in a document. Indeed, the reference to page 145 (in the parenthetic comment above) is a cross reference. Footnotes and endnotes are points in the text stream that refer to additional text, either located on the bottom of the current page or at the end of the chapter or the document, respectively. Lastly, an index references numerous *index entries*, peppered throughout a document, which are used to generate each item in the index. The key point to each of these objects is that once they are created they are updatable and thus remove the tedium of creating and maintaining these structures manually.

Each reference type, except footnotes and endnotes, involves the use of one or more *field codes*. These are special items, formatted as hidden text, that control everything from the structure of a table of contents, to cross references, to the entries that make up an index. For the interested reader, working with these field codes is discussed at the end of this chapter. Their understanding is not mandatory, although in the case of indices, knowing how to edit a field code is a useful skill.

The following table summarizes how references are implemented in Microsoft Word:

Reference Type	Description
Table of Contents	Resolves to a single field code and uses heading styles to create the overall structure. Each heading style (other styles may be used as well) maps to a TOC level which both indicates the style to use within the table of contents, as well as the level of emphasis or indentation (or both).
Table of Figures, Tables, Equations, etc.	Similar to a table of contents except the *caption* assigned to individual objects such as figures, tables, equations, exhibits, and the like are used to generate the table's entries.
Table of Authorities	A special type of table created for the legal profession. This structure references field codes that denote entries such as references to cases, statutes, regulations, etc.
Cross Reference	A field code within the text stream that references the text, page number, section number, etc., for heading styles, bookmarks, footnotes, figures, etc.
Foot and Endnotes	The only reference type that does not resolve to a field code, footnotes appear as auto number entries within the text stream and reference text that appears at the bottom of the page (*not* in the footer). Endnotes are similar except all referenced text appears at the end of the section or the document.
Citations and Bibliographies	Creates in-text citations when your document cites another published work. All citations appear in a Bibliography (which resolves to a field code). Word recognizes a variety of standardized citation formats for Bibliographies.
Index	A single field code specifies the index, while each entry in the index maps to a unique field code placed within the text stream. A document may only contain a single index.

Table of Contents

Word creates a table of contents by associating text in the document which utilize styles of a particular *outline level* with built-in table of contents styles. By default, each of the nine heading styles (Heading 1—Heading 9) map directly to nine built-in table of contents styles (TOC 1—TOC 9). The TOC styles control aspects such as indentation and font size within the table of contents with TOC 1 mapping to the highest level within a TOC and TOC 9 being the lowest. Although the most straightforward way to create a table of contents is to head your chapters, sections, and subsections using the built in Heading styles, you can associate any paragraph style with an outline level. As long as the table of contents is configured to display that outline level (by default a table of contents only recognizes Heading 1 through Heading 3) your custom-tagged styles will appear in the table. Throughout this section, TOC will refer to the Table of Contents while TOC 1 through TOC 9 will refer to one of the nine built-in TOC styles.

Points on Working with a Table of Contents

- A table of contents resolves to a single field code that specifies the number of outline levels to use, among other settings. There is no limit to the number of individual table of contents you can create, thus it is possible to generate a table of contents which is separate from a table of figures, table of tables, etc.

- There are two ways to update a table of contents—update page numbers only or update the entire table of contents. The latter method is used if you make structural changes to headings or add or remove headings.

- If you need to change the formatting within a table of contents, you should modify the desired TOC styles rather than make edits directly to the table. Any edits you make directly will be lost if the table is regenerated. As with many styles, modifying a TOC style can be restricted to the current document, or cascade downward to the document's underlying template.

- Word only searches the text layer in a document when it builds a table of contents. Do not place {TC} field codes or use styled text which has been assigned an outline level inside graphic elements such as text boxes or callouts. Such text will not appear in a TOC.

Marking Text for a TOC Entry

There are three ways to mark text for inclusion into a TOC: (1) You assign a heading in your document to one of the built-in heading styles; (2) assign an outline level to a custom style; or (3) mark text in the document using the **Add text** control. We will address all three methods.

How to Use a Heading Style to Create a TOC Entry

By default, the nine built in heading styles (Heading 1 through Heading 9) map directly to the nine TOC styles. Also by default, a TOC is configured to work with the first three Heading and TOC styles. Changing this option will be discussed on page 150.

Step 1.   Select the text in your document that corresponds to the major units of organization (such as chapter titles).

Step 2.   Apply the **Heading 1** style. Applying styles was discussed on page 33.

Step 3.   Select any text that corresponds to the next lower unit of organization. For example, sub sections within a chapter.

Step 4.   Apply the **Heading 2** style.

Step 5.   Continue working through your document, applying progressively higher
           numbered styles to progressively lower units of organization. You may not
           exceed nine levels of headings.

How to Assign a Custom Style to a TOC Entry

We assume that you have created one or more custom paragraph styles which will be used to mark
units of organization as in the previous procedure.

Step 1.   Open the **Styles** pane (see page 30) and select the desired style.

Step 2.   Right-click on the style (or use the drop down arrow which appears when the
           style is selected) and choose **Modify**.

Step 3.   On the **Modify Style** dialog box, choose **Format**, then choose **Paragraph**.

Step 4.   On the **Indents and Spacing** tab of the **Paragraph** dialog box, select the
           desired **Outline Level**. You may select from one to nine. The outline level will
           correspond to the TOC style of the same number. Example, choosing outline
           Level 3 will cause your custom style to appear in the TOC as if it were styled
           using the built-in **Heading 3** style.

Step 5.   Close each dialog box by choosing **OK**.

How to Mark Text for a TOC Entry

This method circumvents either working with the built-in heading styles or associating a custom
style with an outline level. This approach is problematic. When you mark text in this manner it is
assigned the **Heading 1** through **Heading 3** style (you may only mark text to one of three top
outline levels). Word will modify the style of the marked text and apply the appropriate style, but
oddly may not match the font and paragraph attributes associated with that heading style.
Therefore, because it is possible to have text marked as **Heading 3** using this method, which may
appear differently formatted from text where **Heading 3** was manually applied, this method is not
recommended if a consistent look to a TOC is important.

Step 1.   Select the desired text to be marked as a TOC entry.

Step 2.   From the **References** tab, in the **Table of Contents** group, choose **Add Text**.

Step 3.   Select the desired TOC level from the drop down box (your choices are **Level 1**
           through **Level 3**, or not to show the text in the TOC).

An example of the problem using this method is illustrated below. The entry *Latin and the Early
Printing Press* was marked using this procedure and assigned **Level 3**. The text below it, *Latin and the
Internet* was manually assigned the **Heading 3** style. Both entries are associated with TOC3 in the

table of contents, yet each maintains a different font (both in the TOC and in the body of the document!).

Generating a Table of Contents

You may generate a TOC by either selecting a predefined one from a gallery, or by manually creating one. When a TOC is inserted in a document, Word adds as many paragraphs as required to fully display all TOC entries. After the table has been created, Word will present it as a related block of text. Floating the mouse over the TOC will highlight this block, while clicking once will activate a menu of options at the upper left corner. Word will display each TOC entry in the **Hyperlink** style, although the various indent levels still map to TOC 1 through TOC 9 styles. If you hold down the *Ctrl* key while clicking on a TOC entry you will jump to that location in the document. Using *Alt [left arrow]* will return you to the TOC.

How to Insert a Table of Contents from a Gallery

By default the predefined TOC selections only use **Outline Level 1** through **3**, although this may be modified once the TOC has been created.

Step 1.   Position the insertion point at the location in the document that will display the TOC.

Step 2.   From the **References** tab, in the **Table of Contents** group, select **Table of Contents**, then choose the desired TOC style. A table of contents will appear in your document.

Warning: Do not select the **Manual Table** from the gallery. This inserts a structure that appears like a TOC but is fully manual. You must edit this type of TOC manually. It does not support automatic updating.

How to Insert a Table of Contents Manually

This method offers the greatest flexibility when generating a TOC. If you need to edit an existing TOC the procedure will use the dialog box you work with in this procedure.

Step 1.   Position the insertion point at the location in the document that will display the TOC.

Step 2.   From the **References** tab, in the **Table of Contents** group, select **Table of Contents**, then choose **Insert Table of Contents…**(in Word 2013: **Custom Table of Contents…**). The **Table of Contents** dialog box will appear:

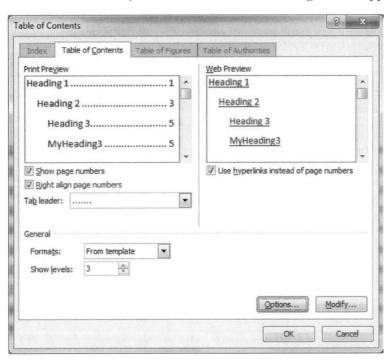

Option	Description
Print Preview / Web Preview	Shows how the current settings will apply for both the printed version as well as an HTML version (should you export the document to that format).
Show Page Numbers	Forces presentation of page numbers in the TOC. Enabled by default.
Right align page numbers	Displays page numbers using a right-align tab stop. By default this tab is placed at the right margin. Enabled by default. If disabled, page numbers appear immediately after the text for each TOC entry.
Tab leader	For right-aligned page numbers, select from a gallery of leading styles or choose *none*.
Formats	Select a series of overall formatting styles (there are more associated with this control than with the gallery of TOC styles). When you choose **From template** (the default), styles are governed by the **TOC 1** through **TOC 9** as well as the **TOC Heading** built-in styles associated with **normal.dotx**.
Show levels	A quick way to set how many TOC levels will appear. For example, if you have text marked using the **Heading 4** style, setting this control to **4** will ensure that those entries appear in the TOC.
Use hyperlinks instead of page numbers	For HTML documents, the TOC is formatted as a series of hyperlinks rather than page numbers (which have no context on a web page). Enabled by default.
Options	Used to assign styles in the document to outline levels. This control is discussed in detail below.
Modify	Used to modify the TOC styles (TOC 1 through TOC 9). This control is discussed in detail below.

Step 3. Make adjustments to your TOC as desired. If you only require three outline levels for your TOC and do not require modification to the existing TOC numbered styles, choose **OK** to create your TOC. This ends the procedure.

Step 4. To associate existing styles in the document with TOC entries, select **Options**. The **Table of Contents Options** dialog will appear:

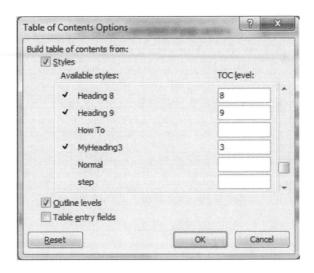

Option	Description
Styles	When enabled (default) Word will associate styles with TOC levels.
Available Styles	Lists all styles in the current document. To associate a style with a TOC level, enter the level number in the text box associated with the desired style. In the illustration above, a custom style named *MyHeading3* is associated with TOC level 3.
TOC Levels	Displays or sets the TOC level for any style in the current document.
Outline Levels	When enabled (default), any outline levels (added when you work in Outline View) are associated with TOC levels.
Table entry fields	Permits the creation of text entries that are not associated with a page number. For example, to break a TOC into major units such as Book 1, Book 2, etc. where these structural levels of organization do not really appear in the document. Their use is discussed in the next procedure.
Reset	Resets all attributes to the general TOC style you choose when the TOC was created.

Step 5.   Make any adjustments to the TOC levels for any style (or built-in heading) that you wish to appear in the TOC. The TOC Level setting will associate the marked style with the TOC style of the same number. Choose **OK** when done.

Step 6.   If you need to modify any of the built-in TOC styles, from the **Table of Contents** dialog box, choose **Modify** (otherwise jump to Step 9). The **Styles** dialog box will appear as follows:

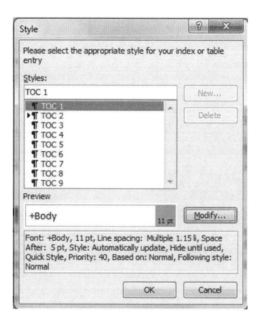

Step 7. Select the style to modify (only TOC 1 through TOC 9 are available), then choose **Modify**

Step 8. Modify the style using the **Modify Style** dialog box. This box was discussed beginning on page 38. Important attributes are related to font, paragraph indentation and spacing (before and after), and tab stops. When you modify a TOC style choose whether to isolate the modification to the current document or store it in the document's template.

Step 9. Step back through the dialog boxes by choosing **OK**. Your modified table of contents will appear in the document.

How to Include Text without Page Numbering in a TOC

There may be situations where you need to include text in a table of contents that does not refer to a page number. In this example, we will establish an entry, *BOOK 1* which will appear ahead of the first TOC entry. To accomplish this, you either select existing text to include, or manually enter it into a form field. If you require multiple tables, for example, a main table of contents along with a separate table of figures and a table of tables, and each requires its own text without page numbering, refer to the procedure beginning on page 159.

Step 1. Select the text in the document that you wish to include in a TOC. Alternatively, enter the text in Step 4 of this procedure.

Step 2.   From the **Insert** tab, in the **Text** group, choose **Quick Parts**, then select **Field…** The **Field** dialog box will appear similar to the following:

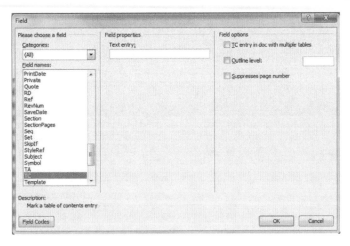

Option	Description
Categories/Field names	Groups document fields by category. If you filter on a particular category the **Field names** control will refresh.
Field Properties	Lists one or more properties associated with the currently selected field. This area may not be available for some fields.
Field Options	As above. Not all fields have properties and the display will change between selected fields to show any associated properties.

Step 3.   From the **Field Names** list, select **TC**. The dialog box will update and will appear similar to the previous illustration.

Step 4.   If you began the procedure without selecting text, type the text you wish to appear in the TOC in the **Text entry** box (in this example we have typed *BOOK 1*). If you selected text it will appear in this control.

Step 5.   Check **Outline level** and indicate the number of the TOC level you wish to use. For example, if this is a major heading in your TOC you would enter *1*. If you intend to add text to group a set of headings at outline level 4, enter a *4*.

Step 6.   Check the **Suppress page numbering** checkbox. Close the dialog box by selecting **OK**.

Step 7.   Repeat this procedure for any other text you wish to mark for the TOC.

Step 8.   When you create the TOC, use the procedure titled *How to Insert a Table of Contents Manually*. Select the **Options** command and check the **Table Entry Fields** check box (illustrated on page 153).

The updated TOC would appear similar to the following. Note that the text *BOOK 1* is part of the TOC field structure but lacks a corresponding page number.

 If working with an existing table, Word may reset the **Table Entry Fields** checkbox when it updates the table. For best results, use this procedure before creating the TOC, or delete the existing TOC after following this procedure and create a new TOC.

How to Update a Table of Contents

There are two options for updating a table of contents. When you update the page numbers only, you are essentially indicating that no new sections have been created in your document, nor have any existing section headings been edited. If you have added, removed, or modified the text in any heading that appears in the TOC, you should choose to update the entire table.

A note of caution. If you manually formatted any part of the TOC, your edits will be lost if you update the entire table. Reformatting a TOC should be done by modifying TOC styles to avoid this situation (see Step 7 of the procedure that begins on page 150 for details).

How you select the TOC and elicit the update command depends upon whether you selected a TOC from the gallery or created the TOC manually.

Step 1.   Select the desired TOC. If you created the TOC manually the fields will appear darkened. If you selected a gallery-based TOC in addition to appearing darkened a small menu control will appear in the upper left corner.

Step 2.   If working without a TOC menu control, right click on the TOC and choose **Update Table** from the shortcut menu. If the TOC menu control is present, select **Update Table...**

Step 3.   Select **Update page numbers only** or **Update entire table**.

Step 4.   Choose **OK**. Word will update the table.

How to Remove a Table of Contents

This procedure is similar to the previous one. If you created the TOC via a gallery, a small menu will appear when the table is selected. Otherwise you must use the **References** tab.

Step 1.   Select the TOC to remove.

Step 2.   If a small menu control appears at the upper left corner, select the drop down button and then select **Remove Table of Contents**. If no menu appears, on the **References** tab, in the **Table of Contents** area, choose **Table of Contents**, then select **Remove Table of Contents**.

 You may also highlight the entire table and press *Delete*, but this procedure ensures that the entire table is deleted whereas a manual deletion may leave field codes present.

How to Modify an Existing Table of Contents

There isn't a direct way to edit a table of contents—no such menu choice exists. However, because a TOC ultimately maps to a single field code, editing it will open the **Table of Contents** dialog.

Step 1.   Select the desired table of contents, then right click on it.

Step 2.   From the shortcut menu, choose **Edit Field**. The **Field** dialog box will appear (illustrated on page 155).

Step 3.   In the **Field names** list, select **TOC**. Select the **Table of Contents** command located in the **Field Properties** area. The **Table of Contents** dialog box will appear.

Step 4.   Make any desired changes using this dialog box. It was introduced on page 150.

Table of Captioned Items

Recall from several previous discussions that it is possible to insert an auto numbering caption that labels a table (see page 120), figures, graphics, exhibits, or equations. The caption is associated with the *Caption* style and this can be used in one of two ways to incorporate captioned items into a table of contents. In the first method, all captioned items appear in a single table of contents. The second method creates a separate table and you would use this approach if you require entries such as a *Table of Figures* or a *Table of Equations*.

How to Include Captions in a Single Table of Contents

This procedure simply associates the **Caption** style with a TOC outline level.

Step 1.   Create a new TOC manually, using the procedure beginning on page 150, or edit an existing TOC using the procedure on page 157.

Step 2.   From the **Table of Contents** dialog box, choose **Options**. The **Table of Contents Options** dialog box will appear (illustrated on page 153).

Step 3.   In the list of **Available Styles**, locate the **Caption** style. Enter a TOC Level number in the **TOC Level** text box. For example, if you want your captioned items to appear lower in outline than the smallest heading, which might be Heading 4, enter a 5 for the outline level.

Step 4.   Create the table or commit the change to the existing table. The captioned items will now appear in the table of contents. An example is illustrated below (captions were given the outline level of 3, in a TOC otherwise only using Heading 1 and Heading 2 styles).

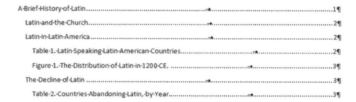

A·Brief·History·of·Latin .... 1¶
Latin·and·the·Church .... 2¶
Latin·in·Latin·America .... 2¶
    Table·1.·Latin·Speaking·Latin·American·Countries .... 2¶
    Figure·1.·The·Distribution·of·Latin·in·1200·CE. .... 3¶
The·Decline·of·Latin .... 3¶
    Table·2.·Countries·Abandoning·Latin,·by·Year .... 3¶

How to Create a Separate TOC for a Caption Type

We previously mentioned that you may caption nearly any type of object in a document, in part because you can create custom captions. For each caption label in use in a document, you may create a table that reflects that caption type. It is not possible to mix caption types within a single table (for example, if you use an *Illustration* and a *Figure* caption label you cannot place these together—you would create a table of illustrations and a table of figures).

Step 1.   Position the insertion point where you wish to create the table.

Step 2.   From the **References** tab, in the **Captions** group, choose **Insert Table of Figures.** The **Table of Figures** dialog box will appear (it is very similar in options to the **Table of Contents** dialog box, discussed on page 150).

Step 3.   Select the desired caption type from the **Caption Label** drop down box.

Step 4.   Make any other format adjustments as required. Choose **OK** when done. An example of two tables, a table of figures and a table of tables, is illustrated below. Each item is a separate table of contents.

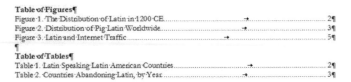
How to Create a Separate TOC for Captions Using a Custom Style

If you associate captioned items with any style other than the built-in **Caption** style, you'll need to follow this procedure instead.

Step 1.   Complete Steps 1-3 from the previous procedure.

Step 2.   Choose **Options**. The **Table of Figures Options** dialog box will appear as follows:

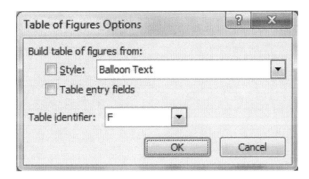

Step 3.   Select the style you use for captions and ensure that the **Style** check box is checked.

Step 4.   If you have text you wish to include without page numbers (see page 154), check **Table entry fields**.

Step 5.   Ensure that the **Table identifier** is *not* set to **C**. If you include text without page numbers in multiple tables of contents, each marked text must be associated with a unique **Table identifier**. (Word reserves the identifier **C** for the first table of contents).

Step 6.   Choose **OK**, and continue with the creation of the table of captioned items.

How to Manage Multiple Table Entry Fields

This is the special case when you create two or more tables and each requires separate marked text that must appear in the table yet must not have a page number (this was first introduced on page 154).

Under this condition the procedure outlined beginning on Page 154 cannot be used. You must manually mark such text entries and also keep track of the unique table identifier. This is a single letter that either Word uses to assign to each table of contents, or that you choose (see the previous procedure). By default, the first TOC is marked **C** by Word. The first Table of Figures is marked **F** while the first table of equations is marked **E**. You may override these assignments but it is generally preferred to allow Word to assign table identifiers.

Step 1.   Select the text you wish to appear in a table (of contents, figures, equations, etc.), or position the insertion point at the location in the document where the marked text should reference, then press *Alt Shift O*. The **Mark Table of Contents Entry** dialog box will appear as follows:

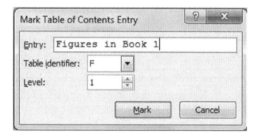

Step 2.   If you did not select existing text in Step 1, type the desired text in the **Entry** text box.

Step 3.   Select the target **Table identifier**. Unless you overrode this option when creating the table, by default the TOC is identified as **C**, a table of figures uses **F**, etc.

Step 4.   Choose the TOC Outline Level by manipulating the **Level** control.

Step 5.   **Mark** the text.

    Each table that displays marked text must have its **Table Entry Fields** property enabled. This property is available by choosing the **Options** button when viewing the **Table of Contents** dialog box.

Table of Authorities

The table of authorities is one of the few objects that Word offers which is unique to the legal profession. Although this book focuses on more generalized documents we will conduct a short tour of how this feature works. Unlike the tables previously discussed which generally base their entries on styles, a table of authorities either depends upon the editor to manually mark entries, or depends on Word to search for text normally found in legal documents. For example, Word will find all occurrences of *v.* since it appears in case citations, and § since it usually appears in citations of code or statute.

Similar to the way captions work, when you mark an entry for a table of authorities, you also select the *category* of the citation. When you create the table, Word can pull all citations across all categories, or you may elect to create individual tables of authorities, one for each category.

How to Mark Entries for a Table of Authorities

Step 1.   Highlight the first entry to cite in your document.

Step 2.   From the **References** tab, in the **Table of Authorities** group, choose **Mark Citation**. The **Mark Citation** dialog box will appear as follows:

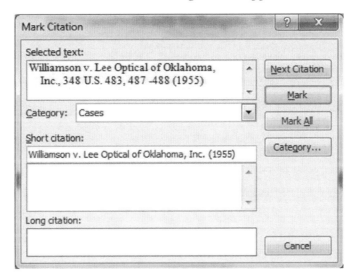

Step 3.   Make any text edits as desired to either the **Selected text** or **Short Citation** text areas.

Step 4.   Choose the appropriate **Category**.

Step 5.   Choose **Mark**. You may choose **Mark All** but only if you are confident that all other entries appear *exactly* as the marked entry does.

Step 6.   Use **Next Citation** if you wish to let Word attempt to locate the next citation, or manually move through your document (keep the **Mark Citation** dialog box open).

Step 7.   Highlight the next citation, then click in the **Selected text** box. Repeat Steps 3 through 5.

Step 8.   Choose **Close** when done.

How to Insert a Table of Authorities

Step 1.   Position the insertion point at the location in your document where the table of authorities will be inserted.

Step 2.   From the **References** tab, in the **Table of Authorities** group, choose **Insert Table of Authorities**. The **Table of Authorities** dialog box will appear:

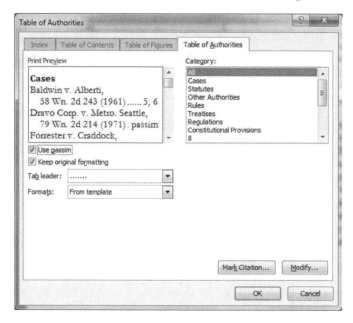

Step 3.   Make adjustments to the format of the table, as desired. To create a table that automatically clusters citations by category, select **All** in the **Category** list area, otherwise to make a table of cases, statutes, etc., choose the desired category. Note that you may not select more than one category at a time.

Step 4.   Choose **OK**. A table of authorities, similar to the following will appear in your document.

Cross References

A cross reference is used anytime you need to refer the reader to a particular location in your document. A very common cross reference is used throughout this book in the form of *See Page XX for details* or *this was previously discussed on Page YY*. The cross reference in these examples is the page number, which points to some object such as a styled heading or a bookmark. If page numbering changes (for example, extra pages are inserted between the cross reference location and the referenced spot) the cross reference updates each time you either (1) print preview the document, (2) close and then reopen the document, or (3) manually force an update.

Word recognizes a number of items that you can cross reference, as outlined in the following procedure. For each reference type you have a choice of what to reference. A common reference is the page number that the referenced item appears on, but you have other choices. These vary depending upon the type of reference. The attributes that you may reference are also explained in the following procedure.

How to Insert a Cross Reference

Step 1.   Position the insertion point at the location in the text stream where you wish to locate a cross reference.

Step 2.   Type any text which may be required. For example, Word only inserts the number of a page and not the text *Page XX* so if inserting a page number, type the word *Page* followed by a space.

Step 3.   On the **References** tab, in the **Captions** group, choose **Cross-reference**. The **Cross-reference** dialog box will appear:

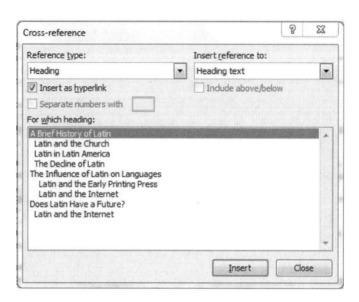

Reference Type	Description
Numbered Item	An item in a numbered list.
Heading	Any location where the built-in styles **Heading 1** through **Heading 9** are used.
Bookmark	A bookmark is a hidden, named point that may be placed anywhere in the text stream.
Footnote/Endnote	Auto numbered text references that appear either at the bottom of a page (footnote) or at the end of the text stream (endnote).
Equation, Figure, Table	Any captioned equation, figure, or table. You must use the **Caption** style to reference any of these objects.

Insert Referenced To	Description
Page #	The page that the referenced object is on. If you use chapter-page numbering, that format will be used.
Paragraph #	For items in a numbered list, this inserts the index number of the paragraph For example, 1A or 2(B)iii. Options include *no context* in which case *2(B)iii* would appear as *iii*, or full context which includes the full reference to paragraph number.
Paragraph Text	For many items that map to a paragraph, this item inserts the full text of the paragraph.
Heading Text	Includes the text of the heading.
Heading #	If using auto numbered headings, the heading number (no context) or if numbered and full context is selected, both the heading number and the heading text.
Foot/Endnote #	The number of the foot or end note (in which case the format is the same as the text) or the formatted number (in which case it appears as a superscript number (very useful when you require multiple references to the same foot or endnote).
Above/Below	Inserts the text *above* or *below* to generally relate the location of the referenced object. For example, *As was discussed in Table XI, **above**.*

Step 4. Select the type of object to reference in the **Reference type** drop down box, then select the nature of the reference from the **Insert Reference to** drop down box.

Step 5. If you uncheck **Insert as Hyperlink** you will not be able to use the cross reference to jump to the referenced point, although the cross reference will still be updatable. Hyperlinks do not appear when a document is printed.

Step 6. To reference only relative position, select **Include above/below**. For page numbering only this inserts the text *on Page* plus the page number. For all other reference types either the text *above* or *below* will appear.

Step 7. Choose **Insert**.

Step 8. To continue adding cross references, keep the dialog box open and position the insertion point at the next cross reference location and repeat Steps 2 through 4. Otherwise, select **Close** to complete the procedure.

How to Insert a Bookmark

Bookmarks are a useful tool when creating cross references. For example you can use bookmarks to refer to specific illustrations in a document where illustrations and graphics may not be captioned (as in this document). Without such bookmarks Word only references illustrations by their caption. You can set a bookmark anywhere in a document (they are hidden objects) and create a cross reference to their location.

Step 1.   Position the insertion point where you wish to create a bookmark.

Step 2.   From the **Insert** tab, in the **Links** group, choose **Bookmark**. The **Bookmark** dialog box will appear:

Step 3.   Enter a name for the bookmark in the **Bookmark name** text area.

Step 4.   Select **Add** to create the bookmark, then **Close**.

 This same dialog box may be used to jump to a bookmark location (first select the target bookmark, then choose **Go To**) or to delete a bookmark.

Footnotes and Endnotes

Foot and endnotes are used to include ancillary text in a document. You may want to provide additional information on a particular point, but not locate it in the text stream. In the case of footnotes, the referenced text appears at the bottom of the page. It is not located in the footer (otherwise it would repeat on each page in the current section with that footer type!). Endnotes appear at the end of the section or the document, although we will discuss how to override this setting as there are cases such as indices and appendices where the endnotes must not be at the absolute document end.

In Word, foot and endnotes both feature auto numbering or auto incrementing numbers or symbols. Both foot and endnotes have a separator that serves to provide a visual isolation between the body text and the foot or endnote. To modify some aspects of foot and endnotes, such as the separator bar, you must be in draft or outline view.

How to Insert a Foot or Endnote

Although there are certain tasks involving foot or endnotes that require you to be in draft or outline view, you may add either reference type while working in print layout view.

Step 1.   Position the insertion point where you wish to insert the foot or end note.

Step 2.   On the **Reference** tab, in the **Footnotes** group, select either **Insert Footnote** or **Insert Endnote**. Word will insert an auto number superscript at the insertion point, then move the focus to either the footnote or endnote area (in the illustration below we are inserting a footnote).

```
consectetuer ·adipiscing ·elit, ·sed ·diam ·nonummy ·nibh ·euismod
laoreet ·dolore ·magna ·aliquam ·erat ·volutpat. ·Ut ·wisi ·enim ·ad
quis ·nostrud ·exerci ·tation ·ullamcorper ·suscipit ·lobortis ·ni
ea ·commodo ·consequat . · ¶
¶
Lorem ·ipsum ·dolor ·sit ·amet, ·consectetuer ·adipiscing ·elit, ·s
nibh ·euismod ·tincidunt ·ut ·laoreet ·dolore ·magna ·aliquam ·erat

[_____]¶
Luptatum ·zzril ·delenit ·augue ·duis ·dolore ·te ·feugait¶
```

Step 3.   Enter the desired text in the footnote or endnote text area.

Step 4.   Return to the document body by placing the insertion point outside of the footnote or endnote area.

How to Set Foot or Endnote Properties

You use the **Footnote and Endnote** dialog box to control how these references are numbered and how they behave within a section.

Step 1.   From the **References** tab, in the **Footnotes** group, choose the **Dialog Expander**. The **Footnote and Endnote** dialog box will appear:

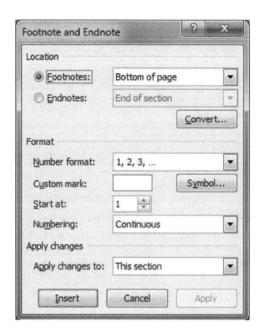

Option	Description
Location	Sets the location option for footnotes (*Bottom of page* or *below text*) or endnotes (*End of section* or *End of document*).
Convert	Forces all footnotes to become endnotes or vice versa. A third option is to swap foot and end notes if the document uses both types.
Number format	Select the desired format for the foot or endnote markers.
Custom mark	Choose a custom mark (this would be for a single foot or endnote you are inserting). If you desire different symbols that auto increment, use the **Number format** control. Alternatively, choose **Symbol** to select a symbol from an installed font library. As long as there is a single character in this field the **Number format** control will appear disabled.
Start at	Set the starting number or symbol for the foot or endnotes. This setting is governed by the **Numbering** and **Apply Changes** options as well.
Numbering	For a document with multiple sections, sets whether numbering is continuous across sections or resets within each section.
Apply Changes	Sets the focus for the settings. Options are *This section* or *Whole document*.
Insert	Inserts a foot or endnote. This closes the dialog box and places the focus in either a foot or endnote.
Apply	Applies any settings you have made.

Step 2.   Make any adjustments as desired, then close the dialog box.

The following table outlines some circumstances common in the publishing industry and the foot or endnote settings necessary to achieve the desired results. Recall from Chapter 4 that chapters are configured by using section breaks.

Common Footnote and Endnote Configurations

Scenario	Requirements
Footnote numbering restarts with each chapter.	In each section of the document, set **Start at** to your beginning number and **Apply Changes** to *This section*.
Endnotes are placed at the end of each chapter.	Follow the instructions above if you wish to restart numbering at each section break. To position the endnotes at the end of a chapter set **Location** to *end of section*.
Endnotes must be placed *before* any index, glossary, appendix, etc.	See the next procedure.

How to Locate Endnotes Before Indices or an Appendix

This is the special case where you wish to locate all endnotes at the end of the document, but you also require an index, glossary, appendix, or other special terminating sections. Endnotes traditionally are located at the end of the body text, so in a situation like this the endnotes must be located *before* items like an index or an appendix. To achieve this result you work first with the **Footnote** dialog box, and then with **Page Setup**.

This procedure assumes that you have created all of your endnotes and that all section breaks are in place, including the one that occurs after the end of the body text and marks the beginning of an index or other special section.

Step 1.   Open the **Footnote** dialog box (see page 167). Use the **Location** control for **Endnotes** and specify *End of section*. Set **Apply changes to** to *Entire Document*. This will position all endnotes at the very end of the document.

Step 2.   Move to the top of the document. From the **Page Layout** tab, in the **Page Setup** group, select the **Dialog Expander** to open the **Page Setup** dialog. Select the **Layout** tab.

Step 3.   For the current section, check **Suppress Endnotes**. Ensure that **Apply to** is set to *This section*.

Step 4.   Move to the next section of the document and repeat Step 3. Continue until you reach the section that constitutes the end of the body of your document. This is the section where endnotes will be located.

Step 5.   Move past the section without suppressed endnotes and continue with Step 3. When you are finished, every section *except* the one that constitutes the end of the body of your document should have endnotes suppressed.

Citations and Bibliographies

These reference items work together in a document. You create citations in places in your text where you need to reference a source (such as a book, journal article, published music, or a website). In this regard, citations are similar to the entries for a table of authorities. Once you have your citations marked (Word inserts text for the citation in the appropriate locations within your document), you create and insert a bibliography. The latter structure then lists all of your cited sources.

There are many styles for the creation of citations and Word recognizes many national and international styles. Unfortunately you cannot create your own citation style for use with this reference feature. Nor may you mix citation styles within a document.

When you create a citation Word stores that information on your computer. The **Manage Sources** dialog box is used to edit or delete any citations you have created, as well as to make it easy to use a citation in several documents. You may also create *Placeholders* which are used to temporarily create a citation in cases where you don't yet have the full citation source. Once a placeholder has been established and is in place in your document, you use the **Manage Sources** dialog to update any placeholder with the actual full citation.

There are three ways to approach citations. You can build a library of citations using the **Manage Sources** utility and then insert citations as needed. A citation may be created on the fly in which case it is automatically appended to the citation sources in the **Source Manager**. Lastly if you do not yet have the full citation you create and insert placeholders then use the **Source Manager** later to update these to a correct citation.

How to Establish a Citation Style

Before you begin adding citations to your document you should select a style to use. As mentioned, you may not apply multiple citation styles to a single document. Citation styles are established by domestic and international organizations and generally apply to specific disciplines. You may need to research the appropriate style authority for a document before working with citations.

Step 1.   On the **References** tab, in the **Citations & Bibliography** group, select the **Style** drop down box.

Step 2.   Choose the desired style from the list. As of Word 2007 the choices fall into the following categories:

Style Standard	Description
APA	American Psychological Association.
Chicago	The Chicago Manual of Style.
GB7714	Standardization Administration of China.
GOST - Name Sort	The Federal Agency of the Russian Federation on Technical Regulating and Metrology.
GOST - Title Sort	The Federal Agency of the Russian Federation on Technical Regulating and Metrology.
Harvard	The Harvard Reference Style.
IEEE	Institute of Electrical and Electronic Engineers.
ISO 690	International Organization for Standardization.
MLA	Modern Language Association.
SIST02	Standards for Information of Science and Technology by Japan Science and Technology Agency.
Turabian	Turabian Style.

How to Create a Citation from Scratch

Use this procedure when you wish to create citations as you create content. If you wish to establish many or all of your citations ahead of time, consult the next procedure.

Step 1.   Position the insertion point where you need to establish a citation.

Step 2.   On the **References** tab, in the **Citations & Bibliography** group, select **Insert Citation**, then choose **Add new source...** The **Create Source** dialog box will appear:

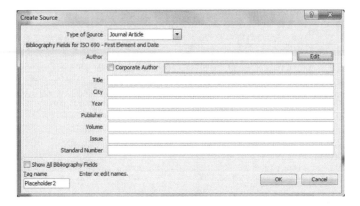

Step 3.   Complete the citation fields as required for your profession (or the standard that your document is to adhere to). Note that the fields may change depending upon which citation style you previously selected. If your citation is tentative or pending, enter a *Placeholder name* in the **Tag Name** field.

Step 4.   Select **OK** when done. Word will insert citation text in the style specified by the **Citation Style** drop down box, as well as enter the citation into the **Source Manager**. An example of an inserted citation, using the ISO 94 style for a book reference, appears below.

```
Lorem ipsum dolor sit amet, consectetue
nibh euismod (Elk, 1974). Tincidunt ut
volutpat. Ut wisi enim ad minim veniam,
```

How to Use the Source Manager

This facility maintains a central store of citations (by default they are stored locally in a file named **Sources.xml**) that may be used to build a citation database for the current document. Alternatively, if your organization maintains a central xml file for a common body of citation sources, you may connect to that source as well.

When one or more citations are transferred to the **Current List** area, those citations are also available when you use the **Insert Citation** tool (discussed following this procedure).

Step 1.   From the **References** tab, in the **Citations & Bibliography** group, select **Manage Sources**. The **Source Manager** will appear, similar to the following:

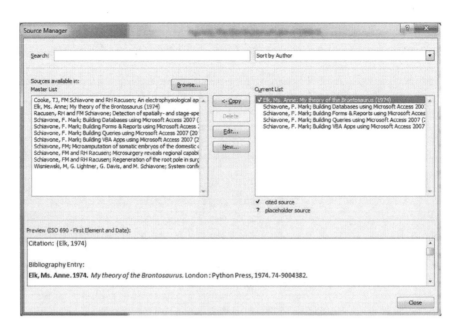

Option	Description
Search	Searches both the master and the current list for an author. Clear any text to return to the full, unfiltered list.
Browse	Connect to another citation data file. The file must be in a particular XML format—there are several vendors and open source websites to refer to.
Master List	Displays the citations in the current master list. By default, this list is stored locally under the name **sources.xml**
Current List	This is the working list of citations for the current document.
Copy Delete Edit New	Use these controls to move, delete, edit, or create citations. The first three manage citations between the master and current list.

Step 2.   Use the following table as a guide to perform specific actions:

Action	Description
Create a citation	Use the **New** button and create a new citation. It will be stored both in the current document and in the master list.
Change data source	Use the **Browse** button if you need to attach to a different citation data source.
Add citations to the current document	First select one or more citation in the master list, then select **Copy**.
Remove citations	To remove from the current document, select one or more citations from the current list, then select **Delete**. Citations are not removed from the master list. To remove a citation from the master list, select from that list, then use **Delete**.
Edit a citation	Select the target citation and choose **Edit**. If you edit a citation that appears in both lists, Word will prompt you to update both lists. Choose **Yes** to update both lists or **No** to only update the list originally selected.

Step 3.   Choose **Close** when done.

How to Add a Citation from the Current List

As mentioned, once one or more citations have been placed in the **Current List** using the **Source Manager**, it is easy to quickly add a citation to your document.

Step 1.   Position the insertion point at the location in your document where the citation should appear.

Step 2.   From the **References** tab, in the **Citations & Bibliography** group, choose **Insert Citation**, then select the desired citation from the list.

Working with Citations in the Document

Once a citation has been inserted in your document, when selected it appears in a small frame that contains a menu. Use this menu to make edits or updates to your citation and/or to the bibliography.

Step 1.   Select the desired citation in your document. When selected it will appear similar to the following:

```
ipsum·dolor·sit·amet,·con
uism    (Elk,·1974)  ·inci
at.·Ut·wisi·enim·ad·minim
```

Step 2.   Choose the drop down arrow associated with the selected citation. The following table explains the menu choices.

Option	Description
Edit citation	Use to add page numbers, or to suppress author, year or title from the citation.
Edit source	Opens the citation in the **Citation Editor**. If you make changes Word will ask if you wish to also update the citation in the master list.
Convert citation to static text	Converts the citation to static text. It will appear in the bibliography but edits to the citation using the **Source Manager** will not automatically update the static text version.
Update citations and bibliography	Refreshes citations and the bibliography.

Step 3.   Make any changes to the selected citation. Position the insertion point anywhere in the text stream to deselect the citation.

How to Add a Bibliography

Once one or more citations have been added to your document, you can create the bibliography.

Step 1.   Position the insertion point at the location where you wish to create a bibliography (in large documents this should necessitate the establishment of a separate section).

Step 2.   From the **References** tab, in the **Citations & Bibliography** group, choose **Bibliography**.

Step 3   Select from the gallery of bibliographies, or choose **Insert Bibliography**. In the latter case an untitled bibliography will appear. In all cases, the bibliography will adhere to the citation style selected (or displayed) using the **Style** drop down on the **Citations & Bibliography** group. An example of an inserted bibliography appears below:

Bibliography

Elk, Ms. Anne. 1974. *My theory of the Brontosaurus.* London : Python Press, 1974. p. 256. 74-9004382.
Schiavone, F. Mark. 2013. *Building Databases using Microsoft Access 2007.* s.l. : Sycamore Technical Press, 2013. p. 151. ISBN 9780615818245.
—. 2013. *Building Forms & Reports using Microsoft Access 2007.* s.l. : Sycamore Technical Press, 2013. p. 256. ISBN 9780615866666.
—. 2013. *Building Queries using Microsoft Access 2007.* s.l. : Sycamore Technical Press, 2013. p. 125. ISBN 9780615827629.
—. 2014. *Building VBA Apps using Microsoft Access 2007.* s.l. : Sycamore Technical Press, 2014. p. 249. ISBN 9780615927114.

Indices

An index is an important navigational tool for readers. Specific points in the document are marked with *Index entries*. Index entries may take many forms in the final index, as outlined in the following table.

Index Style	Example	Description
Simple, single page	Latin, 10 Latin, pig, 25	A simple index entry that cites a word or phrase and the page it references.
Simple, multiple pages	Latin, 10, 15, 22	This style appears when more than one index entry with identical text appear in two or more locations in a document. If two identical entries appear on the same page, Word ignores the second instance.
Cross reference	Pig Latin, *see The Future of Latin*	A cross reference refers to another index entry rather than a page number.
Range	Pig Latin, 4-15	This uses a bookmark that spans the referenced page range.
Main entry with subentries	Latin Counties, 45 History of, 4, 6, 17 Pig, 55	This style utilizes *subentries* which create an indented structure within the index.

Points on Creating an Index

- There are two field types that together work to create an index. Within the text in the document, you insert *index entry* field codes which appear as { XE } when hidden text is revealed. The index itself pulls all index entry fields together into a single structure defined by a {INDEX...} field code.

- Creating an index isn't easy. There are professional indexing services which you may consider employing. If you are up for the challenge, the key to creating a useful index is to index terms not otherwise easily located using the table of contents and to ensure absolute consistency between index entries. A single misspelling in an entry that otherwise references multiple locations in your document will result in two or more individual entries in the index.

- Although both the index entries and the index itself are field codes, the page numbers in an index are not hyperlinks. You'll need to manually jump to the referenced location if you need to edit an index entry field.

- Ideally, the index entries should be created toward the final edit stage of your document. This forces you to focus only on the creation of the index (as opposed to trying to generate new text, edit existing text *and* create index entries).

- A useful technique is to reiterate through the process of marking entries and generating the index. Authors will print out the generated index and proof read the index for mistakes, duplications caused by spelling mistakes, or inconsistent style between the various entries. Once proofed, the author returns to the document and makes edits and corrections directly in the index entry fields. This process may require several cycles to complete the index.

How to Create an Index Entry

Step 1.   Position the insertion point in the document where you wish to place an index mark. To work with existing text, select the word or phrase you wish to mark first, otherwise you will type the entry text manually.

Step 2.   From the **References** tab, in the **Index** group, choose **Mark Entry**. The **Mark Index Entry** dialog box will appear:

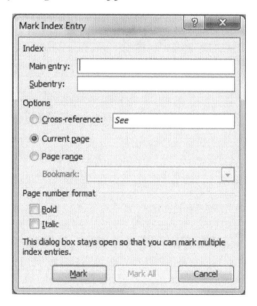

Option	Description
Index	Displays or sets the text for the main entry, and if desired, any subentry.
Options	Controls what the index entry references. For cross reference, enter text in the text box (the term *see* can be changed if desired). The default is **Current Page**, which references the location of the { XE } entry. To reference a range of pages, select the bookmark that contains the desired range.
Page number format	Controls bold and/or italic page numbering.
Mark	Marks the current entry by placing an { XE } field code at the insertion point (or at the end of the text selection).
Mark all	If you began the process by selecting text, Word will add the same index entry for all other occurrences of the selected text in the document.

Step 3.   Create your index entry using the previous table as a guide. For specific types of index entries, consult the following table.

Index Style	Example	Procedure
Simple, single page	Latin, 10 Latin, pig, 25	Place text only in the **Main** text area.
Simple, multiple pages	Latin, 10, 15, 22	As above, except you create multiple index entries, one for each appropriate page. Note that the **Main** text *must* appear exactly the same between occurrences.
Cross reference	Pig Latin, *see The Future of Latin*	Enter text in the **Main** text box, select **Cross Reference**, and then type text that matches another index entry.
Range	Pig Latin, 4-15	Create a bookmark that spans the desired text range in your document (see page 166). Create the text entry, then specify **Page Range** and select the appropriate **Bookmark**.

Main entry with subentries	Latin
	  Counties, 45
	  History of, 4, 6, 17
	  Pig, 55
		For each index entry, be consistent with the text of the **Main entry** (this will map to the "heading" *Latin* in the example. Enter text in the **Subentry**. Note in the example that *History of,* refers to several pages. In this case, three identical index entries were created, one on each referenced page.
		
		If you need to establish a sub-subentry, in the **Subentry** field type the text for the subentry followed by a colon (:) and then the text for the sub-subentry. You can create up to 9 nested levels (although the first level is the text in the **Main Entry** field.

Step 4.   This dialog box remains open after marking an entry. Either close the dialog box or move to the next location in your document that you wish to mark and repeat Step 3.

How to Insert an Index

Like a table of contents, you have some control over the appearance of an index, or you can choose from a gallery of index styles. Also like a table of contents, indices have a set of built-in styles (**Index 1** through **Index 9**) that map to the Main entry (**Index 1**), subentries (**Index 2**), sub-subentries (**Index 3**), and so on. You can modify each of the built-in styles as needed.

If you modify an index by manually inserting text or changing font or paragraph attributes, these may be lost when you update the index (the * MERGEFORMAT and *CHARFORMAT field switches, which apply to several field types, have no effect in the field that specifies an index). To preserve formatting you should modify the desired **Index** styles.

Step 1.   Position the insertion point where you wish to insert an index. Note that you may wish to create a separate section for this purpose. Word will insert a continuous section break by default—to control column structure—but indices generally start on their own page.

Step 2.   From the **References** tab, in the **Index** group, choose **Insert Index**. The **Index** dialog box will appear:

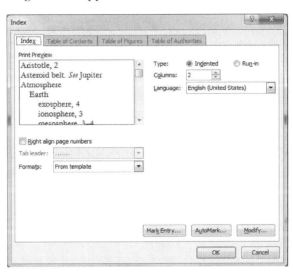

Option	Description
Print Preview	Updates to show how selected changes will affect the final index.
Right align page numbers	Forces page numbers to align to the right. In a multi-column index, numbers align to the right of their containing column. The default is to format numbers a space away from the entry text.
Tab leader	If page numbers are right aligned, you may choose a leading style, if desired.
Formats	Select from a small gallery of built-in styles. The default is *From template*.
Type	Controls whether subentries (and their children) are indented (default), or *Run-in*. In the latter case subentries appear paragraph style in line with the main entry.
Columns	Sets the number of columns. To remove column format set this control to *1*. The default is *2* column.
Language	Specify the language for the index. This is related to any language files you have associated with the document. The default is the default language setting on the local computer.
Mark Entry...	Opens the **Mark Index Entry** dialog, discussed on page 178.
AutoMark...	Prompts for the location of a *Concordance File*, used to automatically generate an index based on the concordance file entries. Concordance files are discussed on page 183.
Modify	Opens the **Modify** dialog box. Use this to make font and/or paragraph changes to any of the built-in index styles (**Index 1** through **Index 9**).

Step 3.   Modify the index settings as desired. Select **OK** to insert the index.

 If you insert an index into a document that lacks index entries (no { XE } codes, Word will insert the following text at the index location: **No index entries found.**

How to Modify an Existing Index

There are two approaches. In the first, you delete the index and follow the previous procedure to essentially rebuild it. Another way is to open the **Index** dialog for the current index and use this procedure.

Step 1.   Position the insertion point somewhere in the index.

Step 2.   Right-click on the index and select **Edit Field** from the shortcut menu. The **Fields** dialog box will appear.

Step 3.   In the **Field Properties** area, choose **Index**. The **Index** dialog box will appear. Follow the previous procedure to make changes to the index, or to manually modify field code switches, select **Field Codes**, then **Options** to see a list of the codes associated with the {INDEX } field code.

Concordance Files

A concordance file is a Word document that contains a list of paired text and phrases that Word uses to automatically generate index entries in a document. The first word or phrase in the pair constitutes the term to search for. It must be an *exact* match to the target text in your document. The second word or phrase in the pair becomes the index entry for the matched term. The paired terms are structured in a two-column table in the concordance file. Each pair occupies a single row in the table with the term to search in the left column and the index entry being inserted in the right column. There should be no other content in the concordance file, which may be named in any manner you choose. An example of the contents of a concordance file are illustrated below.

print preview	Print preview
print preview	Preview, Printing
open page setup	Page setup:Opening
landscape orientation	Page setup: Landscape
portrait orientation	Page setup: Portrait

An index in a document that used the above-illustrated concordance file would appear similar to the following (assuming that each term in the left column matched the text found in the document):

> Page setup¶
>   Landscape, 4, 6¶
>   Opening, 5¶
>   Portrait, 5¶
> Preview, Printing, 4, 5¶
> Print preview, 4, 5¶

Note that the last three entries in the concordance file contain text separated by a colon, thus creating a main heading/sub heading structure in the index. This works because this is exactly the scheme Word uses when creating such an { XE } index entry. Because Word will insert the text on the right-hand column into { XE } fields, as long as you understand the structure of the { XE } entry you can create concordance files that create sophisticated indices.

How to Create and Use a Concordance File

Step 1.   Create a new Word document and insert a blank, 2-column table. This should be the only object in the file.

Step 2.   Built your concordance file by entering search-index entry pairs. The term to search on in a document appears in the left column. On the same row but in the right column enter the text as you wish it to appear in the index.

Step 3.   When your concordance file is complete, close that document and open the document you wish to index auto mark.

Step 4.   On the **References** tab, in the **Index** group, select **Insert Index**.

Step 5.   Select **AutoMark**. A file browser will appear—use it to locate the concordance file you created in Steps 1 and 2. Word will automatically search through the current document and insert index entries where search terms match the concordance file. Insert your index at any time (see the following note box).

You may mix concordance-generated entries with manually-inserted index entries. If you modify and rerun the concordance file, only new matches are inserted. Word will not duplicate index entries.

Working with Field Codes

With the exception of foot and endnotes, all reference objects are mediated by using *fields*. In Word, a field is a special code, only visible when **Show/Hide** is enabled, that appears as a fragment of hidden text contained within curly brackets. For example, to create an index entry in a specific point in a document you insert a field. If the index entry is intended to read *References, about* and refer to a specific page, the field appears as { XE "References, about"} somewhere on the page which introduces *References*. The index itself resolves to a single field code. If a Word document contains a simple index, you can collapse the index and view the underlying field code. For example, { INDEX \c "2" \z "1033"} specifies a 2-column index (\c is a *switch* that in this field code notes the column number) and indicates that the language used will be English-United States (\z is the switch for language and 1033 is the code for American English).

Many users never need to manipulate field codes, but you may find this section useful in order to understand how references really work, or in the specific case of index entries for an index, how to make edits to these codes. See the discussion beginning on page 224 for examples of troubleshooting field colds.

How to View Field Codes

Field codes are inserted into a document as *hidden text*. Unless you instruct Word to unhide this text type fields are not visible in any of the document views.

Step 1.   Select the **Office Button**, then choose **Word Options**.

Step 2.   Move to the **Display** area and in the **Always show these formatting marks on the screen**, choose **Show all formatting marks**.

 Oddly, if you specifically choose **Hidden Text**, it will appear *always*. If you choose **Show all formatting marks**, you can toggle the display to show or hide hidden text and all special markup symbols by toggling **Show/Hide**.

Step 3.   Return to the document. Ensure that **Show/Hide** is enabled by going to the **Paragraph** group on the **Home** tab. The command should be highlighted when enabled, otherwise toggle it by selecting the control.

The Structure of a Field Code

Field codes are always enclosed between a pair of curly brackets { } and are formatted as hidden text. At its simplest, a field code contains a name and nothing else. The field code for a bibliography is simply {BIBLIOGRAPHY}. Another simple example is the field code for a simple index marker: {XE "Latin, History"} which will resolve to an index entry that appears as **Latin, History** followed by the appropriate page number.

The next level of complexity is when a field code includes one or more *switches*. These are single letter codes or words preceded by a backslash. The number of switches a field code recognizes varies greatly—some field codes lack any switches while others may accept 10 or more. The field code for a simple index was previously presented. An example that marks an index entry as a cross reference appears as {XE "Latin, Decline" \t "*See* History"} will appear in the index as **Latin, Decline** *see History.* The \t item is a switch which replaces the page number in the index entry with any text that follows the switch.

Note from the following examples that text which will appear in an entity (in the cases above, in an index) are delimited by quotes. A space separates text from any switch or switches present, and each switch that specifies text is separated by a space and then the text, which if it is to appear in the document in a reference, will be contained within quotes.

Common Reference Field Codes

There are over 80 field codes that Word recognizes. The field codes that are essential to the creation and management of references is much smaller, as the following table explains.

Reference Object Field Codes

Object	Codes
Table of Contents	The table is specified by the {TOC} field while any specially marked text is set using {TC}, otherwise the table of contents entries are based on styles.
Caption	{SEQ } is the field code used for auto sequence numbers
Table of Authorities	The actual table of authorities uses the {TOA} field while each TOA citation is marked using the {TA} field.
Citations & Bibliographies	Each citation uses the {CITATION} field while the bibliography is marked using {BIBLIOGRAPHY}
Index	The index is specified with {INDEX} and each index entry is marked using the { XE } field.

Exploring Field Switches

Word offers a useful tool for exploring which switches (if any) may accompany a particular field. In addition, for fields that specify complex objects, such as {TOC} and {INDEX} this facility is a quick way to return to the dialog box used to create the structure. As indicated in Step 1, not all field codes support editing although there is a work around to open the **Fields** dialog box.

Step 1.   Right click on the field to explore. If **Edit Field** is a menu option, select it. Otherwise, to open the **Fields** dialog box use the **Quick Parts** command located in the **Text** group on the **Insert** tab. Choose **Field**. Either procedure will take you to the **Fields** dialog box, originally illustrated on page 155.

Step 2.   If you were able to use the **Edit Field** command, the field should be selected in the **Field names** list, otherwise use that list to locate and select the desired field.

Step 3.   If the field specifies a complex object, a command button will appear in the **Field Properties** area. If desired, select it to work with the field. Return to the **Fields** dialog box when done.

Step 4.   To view the field codes for the selected field, select **Field Codes**. A text box will appear and display any codes in the currently selected field (if you began with **Edit Field**).

Step 5.   If the field accepts switches, use the **Options** command to open the **Field Options** dialog. This control will list the field-specific switches.

Step 6.   Close the **Fields** dialog box when done.

How to Edit Field Codes

There are several approaches to editing field codes. The first would be to follow the previous procedure and make your edit using the **Fields** dialog box. The more direct approach would be to edit the code directly in the field, as viewed when Word is configured to show hidden text.

To provide a reason why one might need to edit field codes, consider the following snippet from an index:

> Latin, and Internet discussion, 11¶
> Latin, and Internet discussions, 8¶
> Latin, Pig, 9¶

It is more than likely the author intended that the first two index entries appear on one line. The reason they don't is the difference between *discussion* and *discussions* in the two index entries. The way to correct this most easily is to edit one of the { XE } entries directly (the only other approach is to delete one of the index entries and recreate it). In the text, the index entry with the plural form of *discussion* appears as: {XE "Latin, and Internet discussions"}. If the author simply locates this field (you can search on hidden text in field codes using **Find**), removes the *s* from *discussions*, and rebuilds the index (right click on the index and select **Update field)** the corrected index would appear as:

> Latin, and Internet discussion, 8, 11¶
> Latin, Pig, 9¶

When working with indices in particular this is almost certain to be a required task. It is good practice to print out an index and search for problematic entries such as was just illustrated. Return to the document (make sure hidden text is set to be visible) and locate and edit the problematic {XE} field codes.

 Warning: Recall that text within a field code must be enclosed in quotation marks. In the case of an index entry, had the "corrected" { XE } code above lacked a terminating quotation mark Word would treat the entry once again as being different from the correctly-quoted entry, thus reestablishing dual entries for the index topic.

The use of concordance files can greatly reduce the number of errors in { XE } field codes.

Chapter 9 | Multiuser Documents

If you work with two or more individuals who will edit a shared document you will find the topic in this chapter of particular use. Word offers a powerful suite of tools for electronic editing of documents by two or more reviewers. As each individual makes edits, changes formatting, or inserts comments, Word tracks those changes on a reviewer-by-reviewer basis. When the document is returned to the editor or to the document's owner each suggested edit may be reviewed and ultimately either accepted or rejected. While reviewing a marked up document, you may choose what type of edits to view, as well as restrict the view to the actions and comments of a specific reviewer.

You may also protect a document by restricting the styles which may or may not be applied, as well as the nature of actions that a reviewer may take. Word permits you to name individuals exempt from such document protection.

The 2007 and 2010 versions of Microsoft Word are nearly identical in the look and feel of the features we will discuss in this Chapter. In 2013, Microsoft introduced a slightly different appearance but the overall functionality remains the same.

Track Changes

The most commonly used feature for multiuser documents is track changes. When this mode is enabled, actions such as additions or deletions to text, style changes, modifications to tables, and the insertion of comments are tracked. The individual conducting these actions is tracked by reviewer name, and by default, a color that Word automatically assigns (as a reviewer you may choose a color but may not assign specific colors to others).

An example of a fragment of a document with **Track Changes** enabled appears below.

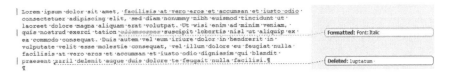

The illustration shows how Word formats inserted text (first line - underlined text), deleted text (second balloon), and format changes (first balloon) provide a visual clue to the edits. The small vertical bars to the left of the text are **Changed Lines** indicators. When reviewing a document with tracked changes, floating the mouse over either a balloon or edited text will cause a tool tip to appear. This tip will announce the reviewer's name, the type of edit, and the date and time of the edit.

 Some document objects, such as captions, may appear to behave oddly when working with **Track Changes**. If an editor deletes an auto numbered caption, until the deletion is accepted it will appear that Word has skipped a numbered caption. Other inconsistencies such as this are introduced when working with **Track Changes** before changes have been accepted or rejected.

In order to understand how track changes works, it is useful to review the **Track Changes Options** dialog box.

How to Set up Track Changes (2007/2010)

Step 1.   From the **Review** tab, on the **Tracking** group, choose **Track Changes**, then select **Change Tracking Options**. The **Track Changes Options** dialog box will appear:

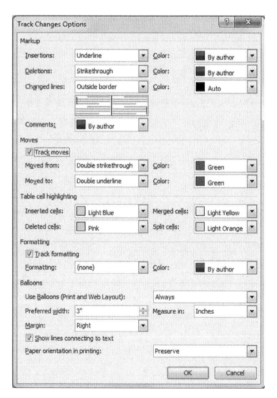

Option	Description
Markup	Set a specific color (or default to automatic color assignment by author) for insertions, deletions, and comments. **Changed lines** applies a vertical line to one of the page borders (if desired) that help to quickly locate changes in a document.
Moves	When enabled, uses the selected colors to note the original and final location for text which has been moved in a document.
Table cell highlighting	Specify the colors to apply when table cells are inserted, deleted, merged, or split.
Formatting	If enabled, you can specify what font attribute and color (such as strikethrough, green) is used to highlight text where a format change has been applied. If **Track formatting** is enabled but **formatting** is set to *None*, Word still tracks format changes but does not use a color or font attribute to mark the changed text.
Balloons	Controls the presence of *Balloons*, which appear at either the left or right margin and cite the review's name and the specific edit action they took. You can turn balloons off or restrict their use to only format changes and comments. Because balloons take up space in a document you may override regular page orientation settings by setting **Paper orientation in printing** to *Auto* or *Force Landscape*.

Step 2.   Make changes to the way track changes are displayed. Note that you may assign specific colors but they will only apply to you and your edits—not that of others. Word automatically assigns a different color to each reviewer.

Step 3.   Choose **OK** when done.

How to Set up Track Changes (2013)

Step 1.   On the **Review** tab, in the **Tracking** area, select the **Dialog Expander**. The **Track Changes Options** dialog box will appear similar to the following:

 Many of the commands available from the **Track Changes Options** dialog are also available from the **Show Markup** and **Reviewing Pane** controls located in the **Tracking** group.

Step 2.   Select **Advanced Options**. The **Advanced Track Changes Options** dialog box will appear similar to that illustrated on page 190.

Step 3.   Proceed with Steps 2 and 3 from the previous procedure.

How to Toggle Track Changes

When track changes is enabled, any edits made to the document by you or another reviewer is tracked. If you make changes to your edits those changes are not tracked (you can delete a tracked addition and the tracking information is also removed). When track changes is off, Word treats edits to the document normally.

Step 1.   On the **Review** tab, in the **Tracking** group, select **Track Changes**, then from the drop down menu, choose **Track Changes**.

Step 2.   Reverse this procedure to disable track changes.

 When **Track Changes** is enabled, the control on the **Tracking** group will appear highlighted.

You can also control track changes from the **Status Bar**. If the term **Track Changes** is not displayed, right click on the **Status Bar** and choose **Track Changes** from the shortcut menu. Clicking alternatively on the **Track Changes** control on the **Status Bar** will enable or disable the mode.

How to Manage Track Change Views

When working with a document managed by multiple reviewers the view can become cluttered, especially if numerous edits have been applied. You can control the view of a tracked document to focus on certain edit types or specific reviewers. Word also offers choices for whether balloons are used to display edits or whether edits appear directly in the document.

Controlling Balloon Visibility

By default, deletions and format changes appear in a call out balloon which appears in the document margin. When you view or print preview the document, Word adds extra width to the document page to accommodate the balloons. When printed, Word maintains the original paper width by compressing the content in the horizontal direction.

The following three illustrations show the options for balloon visibility. Balloons appear slightly different in Word 2013 but the concept remains the same. The default behavior is to use balloons in the right margin to track deletions and format changes. Additions appear as underlined text in the document.

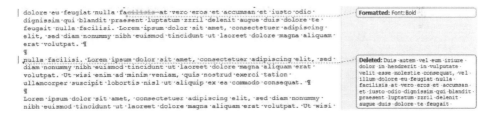

With balloons turned off, format changes appear directly in the document. In addition to the default treatment for insertions (they appear underlined), deletions now appear as strike-through text. In this view there is no extra space added to either the left or right margin:

```
    dolor·in·hendrerit·in·vulputate·velit·esse·molestie·consequat,·vel·illum·
|   dolore·eu·feugiat·nulla·fa̶c̶i̶l̶i̶s̶i̶s̶·at·vero·eros·et·accumsan·et·iusto·odio·
    dignissim·qui·blandit·praesent·luptatum·zzril·delenit·augue·duis·dolore·te·
    feugait·nulla·facilisi.·Lorem·ipsum·dolor·sit·amet,·consectetuer·adipiscing·
    elit,·sed·diam·nonummy·nibh·euismod·tincidunt·ut·laoreet·dolore·magna·aliquam·
    erat·volutpat.·¶
    ¶
    D̶u̶i̶s̶·a̶u̶t̶e̶m̶·v̶e̶l̶·c̶u̶m̶·i̶r̶i̶u̶r̶e̶·d̶o̶l̶o̶r̶·i̶n̶·h̶e̶n̶d̶r̶e̶r̶i̶t̶·i̶n̶·v̶u̶l̶p̶u̶t̶a̶t̶e̶·v̶e̶l̶i̶t̶·e̶s̶s̶e̶·m̶o̶l̶e̶s̶t̶i̶e̶·
    c̶o̶n̶s̶e̶q̶u̶a̶t̶,̶·v̶e̶l̶·i̶l̶l̶u̶m̶·d̶o̶l̶o̶r̶e̶·e̶u̶·f̶e̶u̶g̶i̶a̶t̶·n̶u̶l̶l̶a̶·f̶a̶c̶i̶l̶i̶s̶i̶s̶·a̶t̶·v̶e̶r̶o̶·e̶r̶o̶s̶·e̶t̶·
    a̶c̶c̶u̶m̶s̶a̶n̶·e̶t̶·i̶u̶s̶t̶o̶·o̶d̶i̶o̶·d̶i̶g̶n̶i̶s̶s̶i̶m̶·q̶u̶i̶·b̶l̶a̶n̶d̶i̶t̶·p̶r̶a̶e̶s̶e̶n̶t̶·l̶u̶p̶t̶a̶t̶u̶m̶·z̶z̶r̶i̶l̶·d̶e̶l̶e̶n̶i̶t̶·
    a̶u̶g̶u̶e̶·d̶u̶i̶s̶·d̶o̶l̶o̶r̶e̶·t̶e̶·f̶e̶u̶g̶a̶i̶t̶·nulla·facilisi.·Lorem·ipsum·dolor·sit·amet,·
    consectetuer·adipiscing·elit,·sed·diam·nonummy·nibh·euismod·tincidunt·ut·
```

The third available view keeps the text insertion and deletion changes in the document body while using balloons for format changes and comments:

How to Control Balloon Visibility (2007/2010)

Step 1.   From the **Review** tab, in the **Tracking** area, select **Balloons**.

Option	Description
Show revisions in balloons	Balloons appear in the margin specified when you set up **Track Changes**. Deletions, comments, and format changes are tracked using balloons. When a document with balloons is printed, the text is compressed horizontally to maintain the specified paper width. Insertions appear in the document as colored underlined text.
Show revisions inline	Balloons are not used. Insertions and deletions appear as underlined or strike-through text. Format changes also appear as strike-through text. Comments appear in the text with the reviewer's initials contained within square brackets.
Show only comments and formatting in balloons	As above except comments and format changes appear in balloons.

Step 2.   Select the display option as desired. These changes apply to a document with tracked changes regardless of whether track changes is presently on or off.

How to Control Balloon Visibility (2013)

Step 1.   From the **Tracking** group on the **Review** tab, select the **Dialog Expander**. The **Track Changes Options** dialog box will appear (illustrated on page 192).

Step 2.   Select the appropriate balloon option from the **Balloons in all Markup view show..** drop down box. The options are explained in the table above.

How to Filter Track Change Views by Type or Reviewer

This technique is useful when working with a document that has been edited by several reviewers. You can control what types of markups are displayed, as well as filter by reviewer.

Step 1.   From the **Review** tab, in the **Tracking** area, select **Show Markup**. Choose from among the following options:

Option	Description
Comments	Toggles display of comments.
Ink	Shows **ink** markup (which appear via the **Ink** tool when working with tablets or computers that support this tool).
Insertions and deletions	Alternates between showing these edits as markup or as actual changes to the document. When toggled off, deleted text disappears and inserted text appears in the body without any markup.
Formatting	Toggles markups for formatting and style changes.
Markup area highlight	Controls whether the margin containing balloons appears with a light gray background.
Reviewers	The callout menu lists any reviewers associated with the current document, as well as the default choice *All reviewers*.

Step 2.   To control the display of specific edit types, select the option from the menu to enable or disable that feature. Repeat this step to manage additional edit types.

Step 3.   To restrict the view to one or more reviewers, select the desired author from the list that appears when you select **Reviewers**. Repeat this step to add or remove additional reviewers. To enable the edits and comments from all reviewers, select **All reviewers**.

How to Lock Tracking (2013 Only)

This is a new feature to the 2013 version of Microsoft Word. It differs from the topic of document protection (discussed beginning on page 197) in that a document locked for tracked changes only prevents users from turning track changes off.

Step 1.   From the **Tracking** area on the **Review** tab, choose **Track Changes**, then select **Lock Tracking**.

Step 2.   Enter a password and then reenter it. The password will be required to unlock this feature. Note that if you do not supply a password anyone may unlock the document.

Step 3.   Save the document. When another author opens it they must work with track changes turned on. To turn the feature off, repeat Step 1 and enter the password created in Step 2.

Finalizing a Tracked Document

If you are the owner of a tracked document, you will eventually need to review the comments and edits of the other reviewers and move to accept or reject the proposed changes. You may elect to work with the actions of one reviewer at a time or move to all tracked changes. Additionally, by controlling the type of edit which is visible you can restrict actions to working with a specific edit type. For example, by restricting the view to format changes only, you can step through the document to accept or reject only proposed changes in formatting.

Step 1.   Move to the top of the tracked document and turn tracking off.

Step 2.   To restrict actions to a specific type of tracked change or to a specific reviewer or reviewers, enable or disable the view for each edit type or reviewer. See the previous procedure for details.

Step 3.   On the **Review** tab, in the **Changes** group, choose **Next**. Depending upon any filters you applied in the previous step, Word will locate the first edit which appears. If there are no edits Word will present a dialog box indicating that no edits appear.

 If you apply too many filters such that no track changes are visible, Word will present a dialog box with the message *All tracked changes are currently hidden*. Choose **Show All** to turn off all filters or **Cancel** to abandon the search.

Step 4.   Review the first edit Word finds. To accept the proposed edit select **Accept** from the **Changes** group. To reject the proposed edit, select **Reject**. Word will either incorporate the edit into the document or remove the tracked change, respectively.

The other options are **Accept/Reject and move to next**, or **Accept/Reject All**.

Step 5.   Continue stepping through the tracked changes and repeat Step 4 for each change (if you encounter a comment see the next procedure). To remove a comment, from the **Comments** group, choose **Delete**.

How to Review Comments

Although you can step through edits and comments using the previous procedure, you may also elect to focus on comments as a specific type of reviewer action.

Step 1.   Move to the top of the document and turn tracking off.

Step 2.   On the **Review** tab, in the **Comments** group, choose **Next**.

Step 3.   Review the first comment located (if there are none Word will present a dialog box). To delete the comment, select **Delete**. To edit the comment, right click on the comment (or its balloon) and select **Edit Comment** from the short cut menu.

Step 4.   Select **Next** to move to the next comment. **Previous** will move you back to a prior comment.

Protecting a Document

When you send a document to others for review, you can broadly control what types of actions they may take (such as only adding comments). You may also restrict the styles which may be used in the document. By restricting to a few styles, or restricting all styles, you have control over formatting changes. We will first discuss how to restrict styles from being edited and then move to the general discussion of overall document protection.

When you protect either a style or a document Word prompts you to enter a password. This is optional and if you choose to not specify a password anyone can override your document protection. If you password protect a document and permit some styles or select sections of the document which are exempt from a no-edit rule, then persons granted exemption from the document protection may use those styles and/or edit the document. Giving any reviewer the document protection password gives them full access to control document protection—including specifying a new password.

Warning: If you password protect a document **do not** lose the password! There is no way to recover a lost password and you may need to resort to an action such as copying the entire protected document and pasting it into a blank document to restore edit rights.

How to Restrict Styles

When you permit or restrict one or more styles, you limit the type of style-focused edits that another reviewer may make to your protected document. A protected style may neither be applied nor modified. Permitted styles may be changed, but only to another permitted style. Inexplicably Word offers two methods to protect or permit styles with each offering slightly different options. We will discuss using the **Style Manager** first, followed by the **Protect Document** pane.

How to Restrict or Permit Styles Using Style Manager

When you restrict or permit styles using **Style Manager**, Word will automatically place the document in protective mode when you are done. If you enter a password for document protection, then unless a reviewer knows the password they are truly restricted to the styles you either permit or restrict.

Step 1.   If not visible, open the **Styles** pane by selecting the **Dialog Expander** on the **Styles** group.

Step 2.   On the **Styles Pane**, choose **Manage Styles**. When the **Style Manager** appears, select the **Restrict** tab. The manager will appear similar to the following:

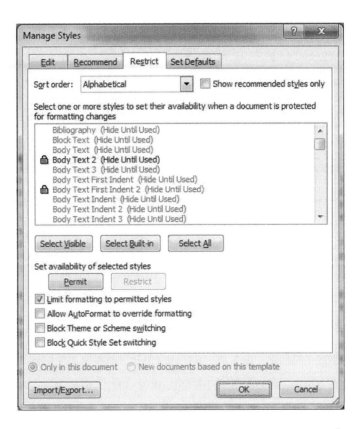

Option	Description
Sort order	Controls how styles appear in the list box.
Select one or more styles...	Use to manually select one or more styles. If you need to select multiple styles hold down the *Ctrl* key while selecting.
Select visible	Selects styles which are configured to appear in the **Style Gallery** or other quick lists. Any such style will be selected in the list box.
Select Built-in	Automatically selects all styles other than any custom styles you have created.
Select All	Selects all styles.
Permit/Restrict	For the selected style or styles, choosing **Permit** will make these styles available for use and modification. Choosing **Restrict** will prevent the use (by a reviewer) or modification of the styles.
Limit formatting to permitted styles	Checked by default. Unchecking this essentially permits all styles to be used and edited.
Allow AutoFormat to override formatting	Permits AutoFormat even when styles have been restricted.
Block Theme or Scheme switching	Prevents reviewers from changing themes.
Block Quick Style Set switching	Prevents users from switching the style sets in the document.

Step 3.   Select the styles to either permit or restrict using one of the selection methods discussed in the previous table, then choose either **Permit** or **Restrict** depending upon your needs. For example, to limit a document to a single style, first choose **Select All**, then **Restrict**. Return to the desired style and select it, then choose **Permit**.

Step 4.   Close the dialog box. Word will prompt you to enter an optional password, and to repeat the password. If you elect to skip this step the document will be protected but any reviewer may simply override the protection. Creating a password restricts the act of unprotecting a document to those with access to the password.

How to Restrict or Permit Styles Using Document Protection

This approach offers fewer choices but still has the effect of noting a style or styles to either restrict or permit in a protected document.

Step 1.   On the **Review** tab in the **Protect** group, choose **Protect Document** (2007/2010) or **Restrict Editing** (2013). The **Restrict Formatting and Editing** pane will appear.

Step 2.   Under the **1. Formatting restrictions** area, check **Limit Formatting to a selection of styles**, then select **Settings…** The **Formatting Restrictions** dialog box will appear:

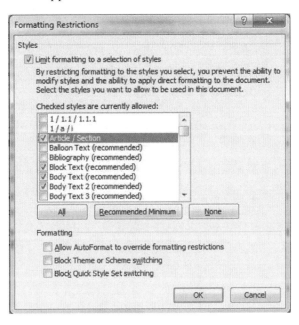

Option	Description
Limit formatting	When checked, enables this feature.
Checked styles are currently allowed	Lists all styles and for styles permitted to be used and/or modified, presents a checked box. You may check or uncheck styles in this list.
All	Checks all styles making all styles available for use and modification.
Recommended minimum	Restricts the selected styles to those in use plus styles that Word reserves for tables and lists.
None	Deselects all styles. In this state no style is available.
Allow AutoFormat to override formatting restrictions	Permits AutoFormat even when styles have been restricted.
Block Theme or Scheme switching	Prevents reviewers from changing themes.
Block Quick Style Set switching	Prevents uses from switching the style sets in the document.

Step 3.   Choose the style or styles you either wish make available by either selecting them individually from the list styles, or by using the selection controls to select all, recommended, or none. For example, to restrict the document to a handful of styles, choose **None**, then manually select individual styles from the list. Only checked styles will be available.

Step 4.   Make any additional restrictions as desired.

Step 5.   Close the dialog box. Note that unlike the previous method the document is not yet protected!

Step 6.   To enforce protection, on the **Restrict Formatting and Editing** pane, select **Yes, Start Enforcing Protection**.

Step 7.   Enter a password and repeat. This step is optional but if you fail to specify a password anyone may override document protection. See Step 4 from the previous procedure for details.

Granting or Denying Edits

You use the **Restrict Formatting and Editing** pane to control the type of edits permitted, as well as to override edit restrictions on a person by person basis. For individuals to show up in the exceptions list, you and the named individuals must be part of a Windows domain.

How to Restrict Edits

This is a simple all-or-none level of control. If you need to override these restrictions to one or more sections of a document, for one or more individuals, follow the procedure which follows.

Step 1. On the **Review** tab in the **Protect** group, choose **Protect Document** (2007/2010) or **Restrict Editing** (2013). The **Restrict Formatting and Editing** pane will appear.

Step 2. Under the **Editing restrictions** area, check **Allow only this type of editing in the document**, then select the desired restriction level from the drop down box.

Option	Description
No changes (Read only)	This is the most restrictive action. The document may only be read by others. No edits, tracking, or additions of comments are permitted.
Tracked changes	Forces the document to enter **Track Changes** when opened by another reviewer. In this mode and without the document protection password, all changes are tracked.
Comments	If selected, a reviewer may only add comments to the document.
Filling in forms	Used when a document contains form fields, a subject which is beyond the scope of this book.

Step 3. Select the desired edit restriction.

Step 4. To enforce protection, on the **Restrict Formatting and Editing** pane, select **Yes, Start Enforcing Protection**.

Step 5. Enter a password and repeat. This step is optional but if you fail to specify a password anyone may override document protection.

How to Create Exceptions for Document Protection

You can choose individuals on a Microsoft Windows domain and grant them full edit access to one or more parts of the document. If you are not part of an organizational network that supports Windows authentication then you are limited to creating an exemption for *Everyone*.

Step 1. Use one of the previous three procedures to open the **Restrict Formatting and Editing** pane.

Step 2. Ensure that in the **Editing Restrictions** area, **Allow only this type of editing in the document** is selected and that an edit restriction (except *Filling in Forms*) is chosen.

Step 3.   In the document, select one or more areas you wish to mark as free edit regions.

Step 4.   Return to the **Restrict Formatting and Editing** pane and in the **Groups** control, select **Everyone**, or choose a group member. If not visible, select **More users** and enter the email or domain\username specification. These individuals must be registered in a Windows domain that your computer is part of.

Step 5.   Repeat Steps 3 and 4 to grant free edit to other regions of the document, if desired.

Working with Exceptions

When you open a protected document where one or more regions have been exempt from edit restrictions, the **Restrict Formatting and Editing** pane will appear similar to the following:

Option	Description
Find Next Region I Can Edit	Skips to the next region in the document where you have permission to edit.
Show All Regions I Can Edit	Highlights all regions in the document where you have permission to edit. The highlighting is a deeper color than that applied if the next control described is selected.
Highlight the regions I can edit	Lightly highlights any region of the document where you have permission to edit.

Turning Document Protection On and Off

If you establish protected styles using the **Style Manager** (discussed on page 198), the document is automatically entered into protection mode. This procedure discusses how to enter and exit protection mode using the **Restrict Formatting and Editing** task pane.

To Enable Document Protection

Step 1.   Open the **Restrict Formatting and Editing** pane.

Step 2.   Create any restrictions and/or exemptions using the previous procedures as a guide.

Step 3.   Select **Yes, Start Enforcing Protection**.

Step 4.   Enter a password to create a password-protected document. If you skip this step, anyone may override your protection settings. The document is now protected.

To Disable Document Protection

Step 1.   Open the **Restrict Formatting and Editing** pane.

Step 2.   Select **Stop Protection**. If the document was not password protected, protection is removed. If a password was applied you must enter it to leave document protection mode.

Chapter 10 | Finalizing the Document

When your complex document has been through production, edits, and reviews you have reached the point where you are ready to conduct the last-minute tasks to prepare it for publication or dissemination. Toward the end of a document's production lifecycle you may find it necessary to embellish it with such elements as watermarks (for example, to mark a document *Internal* or *Confidential*), add page borders, or line numbering. Following these last-minute additions you should have a final checklist and a plan for ensuring that the structure of the document is consistent and free of errors. This is especially true for documents that use references such as a table of contents, cross references, and an index.

We will discuss adding any last minute embellishments first, then focus on a final check list and best practices for publication or dissemination.

Embellishments

An embellishment is an addition to your document that exists outside of the body of text and does not relate to any other part of the document. Watermarks, page borders, and line numbers are examples of embellishments.

Watermarks

For a document that is intended for distribution within a select audience, such as individuals within an organization, a watermark is a useful embellishment that is used to provide a seal or notice concerning the status of the document. Seals may be used to associate the document with ownership by an organization (in the past, this involved the creation of specialty paper for an organization where a seal was either physically embedded within the paper, or preprinted on the paper, used for publication). Presently, it is possible to include an image file in lieu of a watermark image. A text message may be used instead of an image watermark. You may select from stock messages such as *Confidential* or *Do Not Copy*, or create your own custom messages such as *Internal* or *For Use Only by the Office of Management*.

How to Apply a Watermark

You can choose to apply a predefined watermark, create one from a graphic image, or enter a custom text watermark. When creating custom text watermarks you can set a font, font size and color but have few options for placement. In a multi-section document, watermarks are applied to all sections. When a watermark has been applied you choose **Edit watermark** to make edits or modifications.

Step 1. From the **Page Layout** tab (in Word 2013 use the **Design** tab), in the **Page Background** group, select **Watermark**.

Step 2. Select a watermark from the gallery of designs. If you choose this option this ends the procedure. To create a custom watermark, select **Custom watermark…**. The **Printed Watermark** dialog box will appear:

Step 3. Select either **Picture watermark** or **Text watermark**. Use the following table as a guide to the watermark options:

Option	Description
Select picture	Opens a file dialog box which is used to locate the target graphic.
Scale	Set the scaling for the image. The default value, *Auto* lets Word resize the image for the best fit. If you desire a percent increase or decrease in scale enter it directly into the combo box.
Washout	Forces the image to be more opaque than the default setting that Word applies. All watermark graphics are made opaque by default but this setting increases the effect.
Language	For predefined text messages (using the **Text** drop down box), choosing a specific language translates the text. If you provide a custom message this option has no effect.
Text	Choose from a list of predefined messages or enter your own text.
Font / Size / Color	Sets the font, size, and color for the text watermark.
Semitransparent	Similar to **Washout**, when checked (the default), Word makes the text extra opaque. If unchecked, Word simply reduces the opacity.
Layout	Select from a diagonal (bottom left to upper right) or a horizontal (vertically centered) layout.

Step 4.   Select the desired options. If you choose **Apply** you can view the settings with the dialog box open. Choosing **OK** sets the watermark and closes the dialog box.

 To remove a watermark, from the **Watermark** control on the **Page Background** group, choose **Remove watermark**. As was mentioned, to edit an existing watermark, repeat the previous procedure to open the **Printed Watermark** dialog box.

Page Borders

A page border appears in the region reserved for the page margin and is typically set close to the physical paper's edge. Unlike watermarks, page borders may be applied on a section or whole document basis.

How to Apply Page Borders

Step 1.   From the **Page Layout** tab (in Word 2013 use the **Design** tab), in the **Page Background** group, select **Page Borders**. The dialog box will appear:

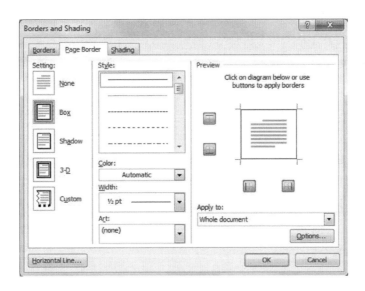

Option	Description
Setting	Use to select a predefined border, a custom border, or to remove any page borders (*None*).
Style	Select line style for the page border.
Color / Width	Set line color and width.
Art	Choose from a gallery of line art styles for the page border. These may be appropriate for certificates and awards and are generally used for single-page documents.
Preview	Displays the effect of any options chosen. The four buttons control the presence of the upper, lower, left, and right page borders, respectively.
Apply to	Sets the scope of the page border. Options are *Whole document*, *This section*, *This section - first page only*, and *This section - all but first page*.
Options	Opens a dialog box used to fine tune the placement of the borders relative to the paper edge or the text area.
Horizontal Line...	Adds a horizontal line to the current page. This control has no effect on page borders.

The **Borders** and **Shading** tabs on the **Borders and Shading** dialog box set attributes for paragraphs and should not be used if you wish to establish page borders.

Step 2.   Adjust border settings as desired, using the previous table as a guide. When finished, select **OK**.

Line Numbering

In a manner that is similar to page borders, Word can apply line numbering to a document in a way that presents the numbers inside of the space reserved for the page margin. Page numbering may be configured to run continuously from the beginning, to reset at each section or for each page. In the latter regard this is the only attribute Word offers that recognizes individual pages as distinct elements.

How to Apply Line Numbering

Step 1.   From the **Page Layout** tab, in the **Page Setup** group, select **Line Numbers**. Use the following table as a guide to the options:

Option	Description
None	Removes any line numbering, if applied.
Continuous	Applies a default line numbering. In this mode numbering will run sequentially across all pages in the document.
Restart Each Page	As above except numbering begins anew with *1* at the top of each page.
Restart Each Section	As above except numbering only resets at the beginning of each section.
Suppress for Current Paragraph	Removes numbering for the current paragraph. Numbering continues below the suppressed paragraph. The lines associated with the paragraph are not counted
Line Numbering Options	Opens the **Page Layout** dialog box.

How to Customize Line Numbering

Step 1.   Follow the previous procedure and select **Line Numbering Options** from the drop down list.

Step 2. On the **Page Setup** dialog, ensure that you are on the **Layout** tab, then select **Line numbering**. The **Line Numbers** dialog will appear:

Option	Description
Add line numbering	Check to enable this feature.
Start at	Set a beginning number. Its scope is dictated by both the **Numbering** setting (see below) and by the choice you made in Step 2.
From text	Sets the position within the left margin relative to the text position.
Count by	Controls the frequency of line numbering. Choosing *1* means every line (blank lines are included) while *5* means every 5th line will have a line number (5, 10, 15, 20, etc.).
Numbering	Controls whether line numbering resets (at each new page or section), or runs continuously from the beginning of where line numbering was established in the document.

Step 3. Adjust settings for line numbering using the previous table as a guide. When done, choose **OK**, then at the **Page Setup** dialog, choose **OK** again.

 To remove line numbering, repeat Steps 1 through 3 and deselect **Add line numbering**.

Final Checklist

Every important document that is intended for distribution to a larger audience should have a formal checklist which is used to maintain quality control. This is especially true for organizations desiring a consistent look and feel among their documents as well as for documents intended for publication.

What follows is a suggested check list. One this author has used over many years and for many publications. It includes some tips on how to leverage features of Microsoft Word to assist in scanning a document when conducting your final checks.

Text and Paragraphs

The first item to check in a document is spelling and grammar, even though Word applies this type of proofing in real time as you type. It is certainly possible for an author to ignore a flagged spelling mistake while instead concentrating on making an important point while writing. When you work with a document that has had several authors this is especially important as authors each have individual styles of generating content.

Two tools are available in Word that make checking text and paragraphs easy: **Spelling** and **Find and Replace**.

How to Use the Spell Checker

By default Word automatically spell and grammar checks as you type. When a spelling or grammar error is flagged (underlined red or green lines) you may right-click and choose an alternative spelling or sentence structure (if available). To force spelling and grammar following this procedure.

Step 1. Position the insertion point at the beginning of the document (you may use the *Ctrl Home* key combination).

Step 2. Move to the **Review** tab and from the **Proofing** group, choose **Spelling & Grammar**. The **Spelling and Grammar** dialog box will appear similar to the following:

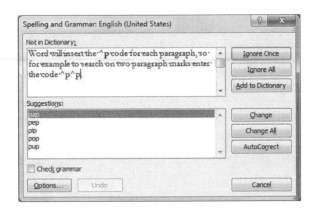

Option	Description
Not in dictionary	Displays the Word which Word believes is misspelled. You may directly edit the misspelled word in this preview area if desired.
Suggestions	Word will display a list of words it believes may be the correct spelling. In some cases Word is unable to locate any suggestions.
Ignore once	If the Word is not misspelled this will force Word to ignore this occurrence only.
Ignore all	As above except Word is forced to ignore all occurrences in the document.
Add to dictionary	Places the flagged word in the current custom dictionary. Word will no longer flag it as misspelled in any document and in fact in some cases Word may suggest this word in the **Suggestions** box for future spell checks.
Change	Changes the word or phrase in the **Not in dictionary** box with the selected term in the **Suggestions** box.
Change All	As above except Word briefly runs a **Find and Replace** operation to replace all occurrences.
AutoCorrect	Adds the term in the **Not in dictionary** area, along with the suggested replacement to the **AutoCorrect** list. When you type the flagged term again Word will automatically replace it with the selected **Suggestion**.
Check grammar	Enables grammar checking while spell checking.
Options	Opens the **Word Options** dialog and displays the **Proofing** page. This dialog is discussed following this procedure.

Step 3.   For each flagged word or phrase, select the appropriate action using the previous table as a guide. Word will continue spell checking (and checking grammar if also enabled) until the entire document has been scanned.

If you start Spell or Grammar checking from some point within the document, when Word reaches the end it will inform you and ask if you wish to continue from the beginning. Once Word reaches the original starting point it will inform you that the document has been scanned.

How to Adjust Spelling and Grammar Settings

There are two ways to get to the **Proofing** area on the **Word Options** dialog. You may use the previous procedure and choose **Options**, or follow these initial steps.

Step 1. Select the **Office Button** (2007/2011) or the **File** menu (2013), then choose **Word Options** (2007/2010) or **Options** (2013). Finally, select **Proofing**. The proofing settings on the **Word Options** dialog will appear similar to the following:

Option	Description
AutoCorrect Options	Enter, edit, or delete AutoCorrect entries as well as set AutoCorrect-specific behaviors.
When correcting spelling...	Make adjustments to how Word spell checks. Use **Custom Dictionaries** to manage dictionaries and/or review the contents of a custom dictionary.
When correcting spelling and grammar...	Controls Word's behavior when checking grammar.

Step 2.   Adjust AutoCorrect, Spelling, and/or Spelling and Grammar settings as desired. Note that these settings apply to all documents, not just the current one.

Step 3.   To exempt an open document from spell checking, select it from the drop down box in the **Exemption for** area.

Step 4.   Use **OK** when done. Any changes will be immediately applied.

How to Use Find

You can use this tool to search for text, fonts, styles, and special characters.

Step 1.   From the keyboard, press *Ctrl F* or from the **Home** tab, in the **Editing** group, choose **Find**.

Step 2.   Type the text to search on and select **Find**, or for more options, select **More**. The **Find** dialog box will expand and appear similar to the following:

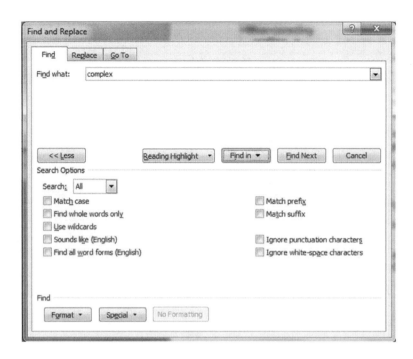

Option	Description
Find what	The word, phrase, search code, or combination thereof to search on.
More / Less	Expands or collapses the **Find** dialog box to show or hide additional features.
Reading Highlight	Highlights the search term in the document. The options are *Highlight all* and *Clear highlighting*.
Find in	Search current selected text, body text or header/footer content.
Find Next	Locates the next occurrence, if applicable.
Search	Options are *All*, *Down*, or *Up*. These are relative to the location of the insertion point in the document.
Match Case	Forces a case match, otherwise Word locates all occurrences regardless of case.
Find whole words only	When checked, Word will not locate your search term unless it is a complete word. For example, *wash* will be found in *washington* when this setting is unchecked but when checked Word will only find *wash* separated by spaces.
Use wildcards	Allows for the use of wildcards. For example, t?p will locate *tip*, *tap*, and *top*.
Sounds like	Uses soundex schemes to locate similar-sounding words. Searching on *Smith* will also find *Smythe*.
Find all word forms	Applies any rules of grammar for the current language to locate additional forms. In English, searching on *is* will also locate *was* and *were*.
Match prefix/suffix	Only finds words where your search term appears at the beginning or ending of a larger word, respectively.
Ignore punctuation characters	Finds words similar to the search term, even if they contain punctuation. For example, *dissolution* would also locate *dis-solution*.
Ignore white space characters	Will locate words with similar spelling yet contain white space. For example, searching on *Jo Anne* will also find *Joanne*.
Format	Use to search on font, style, paragraph, frame, tabs, and highlighting styles. For example you can set up a search where Word looks for all instances of *Times New Roman, bold, 12 pt*. Entering text in the **Find what** would only locate the search text if it also had the correct font attributes.
Special	Opens a menu to select special characters such as paragraph marks, section breaks, hyphens, or wild cards such as any character or any letter.

Option	Description
No formatting	If a format search has been applied using the **Format** command, this removes any specified format search.

Step 3. Apply any search terms and search settings using the previous table as a guide.

You can also establish a search using the **Object Browser** (discussed on page 7). Select the **Object Browser**, then choose **Find**. Specify search terms as discussed above, then close the dialog box. Using the **Previous Object** and **Next Object** controls on the **Object Browser** are like conducting a find operation in the up or down direction, respectively.

How to Use Find to Replace the Object Browser (2013)

It isn't clear why Microsoft decided to do away with the **Object Browser** (introduced on page 7) in the 2013 version of Word. Many of the items the **Object Browser** can search on are still searchable using **Find** (this is true of the 2007 and 2010 versions of Word as well).

Step 1. If the **Navigation Pane** is not visible move to the **View** tab and in the **Show** group, select **Navigation Pane**.

Step 2. In the **Search** bar, select the **Search for more things** drop down box.

Step 3. In order to search on Tables, Figures, Equations, Foot/End notes, or Comments, select the item from the **Find** area.

Step 4. If you need to search on an item not listed (for example, a section break), choose **Advanced Find**. The **Find** dialog box will appear. It is illustrated on page 215.

Step 5. If necessary, choose **More** to make the **Special** command visible.

Step 6. Select the desired object from the **Special** list. For example, select *Section Break* to search on that object type.

You may also open the **Advanced Find** dialog box by choosing **Find** from the **Edit** group on the **Home** tab, then select **Advanced Find**. Begin with Step 5, above.

How to Use Find and Replace

Find and replace is another tab on the **Find** dialog box. When setting up find and replace, the key is to pay attention to whether the **Find** or **Replace** text box has the focus as you adjust settings.

Step 1.   Use the following procedure to open the **Find** dialog, then select the **Replace** tab. Alternatively you can choose **Replace** from the **Editing** group or press *Ctrl H*.

Step 2.   Position the insertion point in the **Find what** text box and enter a term to search on, or if searching on an attribute such as a font or style, expand the dialog box, select **Format** then choose the specific attribute. If the search term is a special character, select it from the **Special** list instead.

Step 3.   Move the insertion point to the **Replace with** text box. Type the replacement term, or if replacing format attributes, choose **Format** and again select the replacement attributes. If the replacement involves a special character, select **Special** instead.

Step 4.   Step through the document using the **Find** or **Find Next** command, then choosing **Replace** or to skip a replacement, **Find** or **Find Next**.

Example: Replace Double Paragraph Marks with Singles

As an example, we will search a document and replace any occurrence of double paragraph marks with a single paragraph mark. This would be to clean up poor data entry where a typist used double paragraph marks to isolate one paragraph from the next (a style should be used instead that takes advantage of the **Space Before** and **Space After** paragraph attributes). Because there may be legitimate instances of double paragraph marks it is recommended that this search be conducted manually and not use the **Replace all** command.

Step 1.   Open the **Replace** dialog box. Position the insertion point in the **Find what** text area.

Step 2.   If necessary, select **More**, then **Special**. Select **Paragraph Mark** from the list. Word will insert the code **^p** in the search box. Repeat this Step or simply type another **^p** code (no space between codes unless you need to search on paragraph-space-paragraph mark). Note that this code could be manually typed in the **Find what** text area (the ^ symbol is *Shift 6* on the keyboard).

Step 3.   Position the insertion point in the **Replace with** text area. Type **^p** or use the **Special** command to select **Paragraph Mark**.

Step 4.   Conduct the search and replace operation. The focus is on removing any second paragraph marks used to separate paragraphs.

Example: Replace the Calibri Font with Arial

These are two sans-serif fonts. Calibri is Microsoft's version of the ITC Arial font. In this example, if you only specify font name all instances will be replaced. If you select Calibri 24 pt. then only text with that font and font size will be replaced. Here, we will not enter any search terms. The effect will be to globally replace the Calibri font with Arial, regardless of the font size or other font attributes. The text in each replacement will remain and only the font will change.

Of course this type of operation should be conducted by modifying a style, but is also useful if you've discovered that a colleague has manually applied font attributes rather than work with styles.

Step 1.   Open the **Replace** dialog box. Position the insertion point in the **Find what** text area.

Step 2.   If necessary, select **More**, then **Format**. From the menu, select **Font**.

Step 3.   In the **Font** dialog box, only select the font *Calibri*. Close the dialog box.

Step 4.   Position the insertion point in the **Replace with** text area. Repeat Steps 2 and 3 but select the font *Arial*.

Step 5.   Conduct the search and replace operation.

 Warning: When you either find or find and replace on a format attribute, the attribute will appear under the **Find what** and/or **Replace with** text boxes. Remember to select **Remove formatting** when done, or when beginning another search or else these settings will remain in effect until Word is shut down and restarted!

Points on Text and Paragraphs

- When spell and/or grammar checking a document, begin at the top of the document and move downward. Word will ensure that the entire document is scanned in the event you begin elsewhere, but a formal, top-to-bottom approach seems to elevate the importance of running such a check. If you need to jump past an area such as the table of contents, reposition the insertion point below the area to skip and restart spelling and/or grammar checking.

- When Word encounters a technical term and flags it as misspelled, add it to your custom dictionary. If you need to edit this dictionary, it is available from the **Office button**. Select **Word Options**, then **Proofing**. Choose **Custom Dictionaries** and select the dictionary to edit, then select **Edit word list**. Be aware that the default custom dictionary is shared by all members of the Microsoft Office Suite.

- A common problem, especially when working with several authors, is the use of a single or double space following a sentence end, as well as the use of two carriage returns (***Enter*** key) to add space between paragraphs. In the former case, use **Find and Replace** to step through the document and apply a consistent number of spaces following the end of each sentence. Replacing double paragraph marks was the subject of a previous procedure.

- Many organizations apply rules to control how letter-space-number combinations are treated. To prevent a letter-space-number from breaking at the end of a line (thus leaving the number alone to start the next line), replace the space with a non-breaking one. When typing text, this is accomplished by using the *Shift Ctrl Space* key combination. When finalizing a document, use **Find** to search for any letter, space, or number and manually replace the space with a non-breaking one.

- It is common for authors to use the en-dash (-) when an em-dash (—) is grammatically required. You can use **Find and Replace** to conduct this operation. When creating text, insert such characters by selecting **Symbol** from the **Symbols** group on the **Insert** tab. Choose **More symbols…**, then choose the **Special Characters** tab and select the desired character. Word will associate a keystroke combination for each character. Example, using *Alt Ctrl Num—* will insert an em-dash (Num— means the dash associated with the numeric keypad).

Styles

When working with a document that features custom styles it is important to ensure that styles have been consistently applied though the document. In addition, if you use the **Apply Styles** dialog box to switch between styles (discussed on page 32) an unnoticed misspelling of a style name causes Word to create a new style! Thus careful inspection of the styles used in the document is part of a comprehensive checklist.

Searching for Styles

There are two approaches to this type of operation. You can open any of the style dialog boxes and manually move through the document. Positioning the insertion point within any paragraph will cause any of these dialogs or panes to display the style enforced at that point. In this way you can check to verify that the correct style is being used at specific locations.

Another approach is to search on a given style. To do this, configure the **Find** dialog (or use the Object Browser as discussed in the note box on page 218) and use the **Format** command, then select **Styles**. Choose the style to search on. This technique is useful to locate styles which should not be in the document. For example, a document that does not use the **Normal** style should be searched to ensure that this style is not located anywhere in the document.

Tables, Figures, and Other Elements

It is important that the tables, figures, equations, and other inserted objects in your document be consistently placed and formatted. There are several tricks you can employ in this regard. For figures, graphics, equations, and other elements you can define styles that control their placement in the text stream and also the amount of blank space to be allocated before and after the element. Once defined it is a simple matter of using the **Object Browser** to locate each item. With one of the style dialog boxes open you can then check to ensure that the correct style is being applied. It gets a bit touchier if you embed these elements inside a text box (for example to control text flow). Here you must manually inspect the properties of each text box to ensure that, whatever your formatting needs, these elements are being consistently treated.

Regarding tables, another best practice is to create a table and format it according to your needs, then either save the table in an otherwise blank document or save the design as a **Building Block**. If you save the table as a separate file, each time you need to insert a copy you use the **Text from file** command (**Insert** tab, **Text** group—choose **Object**, then select **Text from file**). If working with a **Building Block**, refer to page 106 and ensure that you save the table design into the **Tables** gallery. Remember too that the **Object Browser** can search for each instance of a table, thus making it easy to step through a document to inspect each table.

Sections

Another task is to ensure that section breaks occur in the correct location to establish each section, that they are of the correct type and that each section has the appropriate section-specific settings applied. There are two quick methods for moving through sections:

- If sections begin with text using the **Heading 1** style, use the **Document Map** (discussed on page 6) to move between sections. As you move through the document, pay attention to the section number displayed in the **Status Bar**.

- A second approach is to use the **Object Browser** and **Browse by Section** (in Word 2013 use **Advanced Find** and search on section breaks which are on the **Special** menu).

In either case, once in a particular section, open the **Page Setup** dialog (page 56) and verify that the correct section-specific attributes are being applied.

Header and Footers

As a special case, the headers and footers in a multi-section document must be inspected, especially if they are configured to be different between sections. As was discussed on page 86 in the troubleshooting headers and footers section, it's best to conduct a review of headers and footers by beginning at the bottom of the document and moving upward. Ensure that for sections that need to be unique the **Same as Previous** attribute is not enabled. Recall too that for the most complex type of section headers and/or footers (different first page, different odd and even pages), you must have three separate headers and footers within each section. These must be inspected individually and on a section-by-section basis.

As a quick first pass for such inspections, you can work in **Print Layout** view with the **Document Map** open (or **Browse by Section** using the **Object Browser**) and inspect the headers and footers across your section (or chapter) breaks. Since all odd page footers within a long section are really specified by a single footer, you only need to verify that the first couple of pages *at the beginning* of each section are formatted correctly.

References

There are several considerations when working with references. Chapter 8 extolled the virtues of using these automatically-updatable field codes yet there are important implications when you conduct last minute edits. For example, unless you specifically force field codes to update, they only automatically update when the document is first opened. If you open the final version of a document, make a last minute change that effects pagination, save the document but then keep it open, neither the open version, the version saved, nor the printed version of the opened document have up-to-date references! The document will not automatically update until it is opened again. We will discuss update options in a moment.

The other consideration is when a reference link breaks. This can happen if you delete a bookmark or a section heading that was the target for a cross reference or a table of contents entry. We will discuss how to locate and fix these broken links as well.

Update Options

Since Word only updates reference fields when a document is first opened, any edits that may affect references will not be updated until the document is closed and reopened, unless you force an update. There are several approaches:

- Force an individual field code to update by right-clicking on it and selecting **Update Field**. For a table of contents, you will be prompted to either update the page numbers or the entire table. Choose the latter if there have been any changes to the headings in the document. For cross references, indices and the like, the field will update without any prompts.

- Force updates across the entire document. Select the entire document (*Ctrl A*, or triple-click in the right margin, or choose **Select all** from the **Select** command on the **Editing** group). Once the entire document has been selected, press *F9*. If one or more tables of contents are present, you will be prompted as above.

- Set printing so fields are updated before the document is printed. Open the **Word Options** dialog (**Office** button, then choose **Word Options**). Move to the **Display** area and in the **Printing Options** section, check **Update fields before printing**.

In any event, before finalizing a document you should also search for broken field references.

Broken References

A broken reference occurs when the item a reference points to is deleted or modified such that Word can no longer resolve the link. Breaks typically occur in cross references that use bookmarks but may also appear in a table of contents. The following illustration shows how a broken cross reference appears in a document. In this case the reference pointed to a bookmark which was subsequently removed.

```
erat ·volutpat. ·¶
Duis ·autem ·vel ·eum · (See ·page ·Error! ·Bookmark ·not ·defined.) ·iriu:
hendrerit ·in ·vulputate ·velit ·esse ·molestie ·consequat, ·vel ·illum
```

If a document contains one or more broken links, Word only informs you by placing the *Error!* message in the problematic field code. Luckily these error messages appear in the document regardless of whether **Show/Hide** is enabled and regardless of the view. Still, you must search through the document to locate and address any broken references.

Points on Broken References

- If you receive an *Error!* message within a table of contents, rebuild the entire table. Also ensure that you are not in **Track Changes** mode and that if the document had been tracked, that all edits have been either accepted or rejected, then rebuild the table. Remember that if your document has multiple tables of contents the insertion point should be in the problem table before rebuilding.

- Errors in an index are rare because an index only references { XE } codes, whereas a table of contents uses internal bookmarks generated by Word. Nonetheless, if you receive an error message within an index, rebuild the index. Again, if the document had been tracked ensure that all edits have been accepted or rejected first, turn tracking off, then rebuild the index.

- Use **Find** to locate any parts of the document containing the *Error!* message. The following procedure will help diagnose problems with cross references.

How to Diagnose Cross Reference Errors

Broken page references nearly always involve a bookmark or a heading that has been deleted.

Step 1.   To determine the name of the bad bookmark, right click on the ***Error!*** message and choose **Toggle Field Code**. The bookmark will appear directly in the field. Example: { PAGEREF PigLatin \h } where PigLatin is the name of the missing bookmark. If you select the second option the **Fields** dialog box will appear.

Step 2.   If it is a simple matter of editing the bookmark name, you may directly edit the field code. Once done, right click on the field code and select **Update field** from the shortcut menu.

Step 3.   If you choose not to directly edit the field code you must modify the field to point to another bookmark, header, or other valid reference point in the document or add a new bookmark. Use the following table as a guide.

Option	Description
Add a new bookmark	Move to the area of the document your broken reference should point to and insert a new bookmark (see page 166). Return to the broken reference, delete the field, and recreate the cross reference (see page 163).
Change what the cross reference point to	Since a cross reference may also point to any heading, numbered item, or captioned table, figure, or equation, you may find it easier to point to some other anchor in your document. To accomplish this, delete the existing field and recreate the cross reference (see page 163).

Print Ready

The final review should involve checking the document both as it will appear when printed and obviously after printing. The latter is an important point. As much as we'd like to claim that our offices are moving toward being paperless, many editors know that many classes of typographical errors just don't seem to get noticed unless they appear on a physical piece of paper. *Th fct tht yu cn undrstnd ths pasage* speaks to the human mind's ability to correct misspelled words. Thus print review should occupy two separate actions—the first using **Print Preview** to check pagination and other large-scale issues and the second being a careful proofreading of the printed document. We'll address the first procedure here.

Using Print Preview

This view is generated using settings Windows derives from the currently-selected printer. Ensure that the desired printer has been selected, or if formatting a book for publication, you should simply check to make sure the printer you generally work with locally or on your network is currently selected.

Step 1.   To check the current printer, from the **Office** button (2007/2010) or from the **File** menu (2013), choose **Print**, and from the sub menu, select **Print**. On the **Printer** dialog box, verify that the correct printer is displayed in the **Name** drop down box. If so, choose **Cancel**. If not, select the target printer, then choose **Close**. (Choosing **OK** will send the document to the printer!)

Step 2.   Return to the **Office** button and again select **Print**. From the sub menu choose **Print Preview**. The document will appear in print preview mode.

Step 3.   To inspect pagination, either select **Two pages** from the **Zoom** group on the **Print Preview** tab, or select **Zoom**, then **Many Pages** and select the number of pages to view at once.

Step 4.   Step through the document, paying special attention to pages immediately before and after each section break, especially if you are utilizing different odd/even headers and footers, or different first page headers and footers.

Step 5.   Continue your review until all pages have been inspected. Close **Print Preview** when done.

 Another useful view is **Full Screen Reading** which emulates print preview but also supports some editing of the document. Select this view from the view controls located on the lower right **Status Bar**, or choose it from the **View** tab, **Document Views** group.

Index

About the Author

F. Mark Schiavone was originally trained as a research scientist, and in that capacity he began constructing database applications, analyzing complex data sets, and authoring technical publications over 30 years ago. Since then he has designed and delivered over 30 software training titles to clients in large to mid-size organizations, including the US Department of Education, the National Weather Service, and the International Monetary Fund in topics such as Microsoft Access, Microsoft Word, Microsoft Excel, and in the VBA programming language. He also has 8 years' experience in public finance, capital project planning, and local government budgeting and has constructed numerous database applications to support those endeavors.

Along with his partner John he has restored three stone houses (two of which were 18th century while the most recent house dates from 1835), reroofed a loafing barn, disassembled and reassembled a corn crib, and built several frame houses, additions or outbuildings. He has designed every new structure built on his property. He is a passionate all weather, high mileage motorcyclist and is usually the only motorcyclist on the local roads when the temperature is below 25° F.

Printed in Great Britain
by Amazon.co.uk, Ltd.,
Marston Gate.